FOUR TERRIFIC WAYS
TO CUT YOUR FOOD BUDGET
WITH TASTY HOT DOG RECIPES

1) *The Snappy Frank Sandwich*
   (French roll, chili sauce, steamed frankfurter, hot sauerkraut and caraway seeds)

2) *Hot Diggity Hot Dog Sandwich*
   (Pumpernickel, tangy mustard, cooked frankfurter and cole slaw)

3) *Hot Dogs and Beans on a Bun*
   (Vegetarian beans, catsup, mild mustard, brown sugar, lemon juice and cooked frankfurter on split hot dog buns)

4) *Just Plain or Fancy Frank*
   (Cooked frankfurter plain or with trimmings: relish, mustard, tomato, cucumber, cheddar cheese, red onion rings, hot peppers or crisp bacon)

Just a few food cost-cutting delights from

THE WALTON FAMILY COOKBOOK

The Walton Family Cookbook

BY SYLVIA RESNICK

Inspired by the top-rated television series created by Earl Hamner, Jr.

The information in the book is based upon interviews dating back to 1975.

Published in the USA by:
BearManor Media
PO Box 1129
Duncan, Oklahoma 73534-1129
www.bearmanormedia.com

ISBN 978-1-59393-269-5

Printed in the United States of America.

To Max and Barry with my loving appreciation for being such good sports about eating most of their meals out during the months I worked on this cookbook.

Contents

Introduction

Fans of television's "The Waltons" are familiar with the scenes showing the members of the Walton family gathered around the kitchen table. Mealtime is an integral part of just about every episode. It's a time of day when families meet not only to enjoy mom's good cooking, but also to enjoy one another. Perhaps part of the appeal of this very popular series is due to scenes such as those where the family unity is emphasized.

In a recent sociological study at The Jesuit Center for Social Studies mealtime underwent considerable analysis. What emerged is the fact that not only does the family that prays together stay together, but the family that eats at least one meal together tends to do the same. Family mealtime is a time for sharing; a time for getting to know one another in a relaxed atmosphere. Mealtime should be a happy time. As we see it depicted on the Waltons it is just that.

Talking over the events of the day; sharing kitchen duties; enjoying the good food prepared by the cook (better known as mom) in the house is a very basic part of family life. The members of "The Waltons" each have their own favorite dishes as well as memories of family mealtime that they look happily back upon.

1

Appetizers

*"A good appetizer should whet the palate
in preparation for the meal to follow."*

---

*Appetizers vary as widely as appetites do. They
range from the very simple—just something to take
the edge off gnawing hunger while waiting for dinner
to be served—to the more elaborate appetizer that
can serve as a light meal in itself.*

*An appetizer can be served at the table just be-
fore the main course, during those last few moments
of preparation. It can be served in the living room
accompanied by cocktails or a before-dinner aperitif
when there are guests for dinner; buffet style or à la
smorgasbord on a sideboard or tea cart in the dining
room; or, as is the favorite of many of the Waltons,
on the patio, as the weather in Southern California
is conducive to patio dining.*

ELLEN CORBY, *who plays Grandma Walton, says
that she just naturally gravitates toward Danish
food. Her parents and grandparents were born in*

1

Copenhagen. *Ellen, whose maiden name was Hansen, spent a great deal of time in her mother's restaurant when she was in high school. She waited on tables at night in between doing her schoolwork and rehearsing for the numerous plays in which she appeared. (Ellen has been involved in one form or other of theater since early girlhood.)*

"*I was the richest kid in high school,*" *she says,* "*because I made so much money in tips. I always told people that I didn't get any salary (the truth), so I would always get the tips. That was before the depression. We had a very good business in Philadelphia and then we lost everything and headed for California.*

"*But my mother was a fabulous cook and did all of the baking. We always had a blue-plate special that was a Danish dish and it was something different every night.*"

The Danes have a way of making even the most inexpensive and simplest dishes look and taste delicious. Their reputation for tempting smorgasbord spreads is almost unbeatable. After nibbling on some of these tempting, appetite-whetting specialties the hungriest of your guests and family will wait more patiently for dinner.

Farsetter, *or forcemeat, is the basis for many Danish dishes, both main course and appetizers. It is one of Ellen's favorite foods.*

Farsetter

1 pound veal	1 pint milk, boiled and
Salt to taste	chilled
1 egg, well beaten	Pepper to taste
2½ ounces flour (approx.	1-2 teaspoons grated onion
⅓ cup)	

Mince the meat finely in a meat grinder or blender. Transfer to large bowl. Add salt and work in egg using a pounding motion. Add flour and work in well with hands. Add a few drops of cold water, then slowly add milk as you continue to work with meat mixture, blending in well. Season with pepper, and add grated onion. Taste and add more salt, if needed.

Danish Style Stuffed Cabbage With Forcemeat

1 large firm head cabbage
3 tablespoons sweet butter, melted

Remove outer leaves. Slice off a thin piece of cabbage at stalk end to serve as a lid after stuffing. With a sharp knife hollow out cabbage leaving a sufficient layer of leaves to fill with forcemeat. Fill and replace lid.

Tie a clean piece of cheesecloth around cabbage and simmer in lightly salted boiling water for about 3 hours. Drain well in a colander. Remove stuffed cabbage to a hot plate. Pour the melted butter over stuffed cabbage. Slice as you would a cake and serve hot on cake plates. (Serves 4)

Although Ellen was very busy with her theater work her mother did manage to get her into the restaurant's kitchen once in a while and that's how Ellen learned to cook and to perfect her own specialties. "Today," she says, "I prefer good wholesome food. I stay healthy that way. Simplicity is the key word. One thing I learned at the restaurant that has come in very handy on the television show is how to handle dishes. Sometimes when we're doing a kitchen scene on 'The Waltons,' I feel like I'm back in my mother's restaurant."

Some of the easy-to-prepare smorgasbord specialties that repeat customers always ordered were the ones Ellen mastered early in her culinary endeavors.

Open-Faced Sandwiches

6 slices very thin pumpernickel bread, lightly buttered

6 lettuce leaves, well rinsed and drained on paper towels (in Ellen's day they used clean linen napkins)

6 sliver thin slices of your favorite Danish cheese

Mild mustard

6 thin slices tomato

Garlic salt (optional)

Parsley sprigs

Top each slice of bread with a lettuce leaf, then add cheese and spread lightly with mustard. Add tomato and a dash garlic salt. Arrange on a lettuce-lined platter and decorate with parsley. (Serves 2-3, depending on how hungry they are)

Special Shrimp Appetizer

6 slices party rye
Lettuce
18 baby shrimp
Mayonnaise
Hard-cooked egg yoke
Lemon wedges

Butter the bread. On each slice place a lettuce leaf, 3 shrimp and a dab of mayonnaise. Decorate each with a sprinkle of egg yolk that has been put through a sieve. Serve icy cold garnished with wedges of lemon. (Serves 6)

JON WALMSLEY *(Jason) has a passion for yogurt. He likes it so much he eats yogurt as often as three times a day. Since it's a high protein food, it may account for the energy level he maintains.*

You've seen Jon playing the harmonica and the guitar on "The Waltons," but he is a truly talented young man in just about every phase of music. He plays seven musical instruments, has a good singing voice and is also a composer (all this in his "spare" time when he's not in front of the cameras).

An only child, Jon is very close to his parents. He's learning to cook with the patient assistance and guidance of his mother. Mr. Walmsley, a good cook himself, often takes over in the kitchen to give Mrs. Walmsley a night off. Although Jon claims that he's gotten no further than fixing a sandwich for himself and has really only just learned to boil water, he thinks he may try his hand at this recipe he recently saw in a magazine. One of the ingredients is yogurt, wouldn't you know it.

Appetizing Meatballs

1 pound ground beef	½ teaspoon thyme
1 envelope onion soup mix	½ teaspoon oregano
¼-½ cup fine cracker crumbs	Salt to taste
	Cooking oil
	Paprika (optional)

1   8-ounce carton plain yogurt

Mix beef with half of the onion soup mix, cracker crumbs, herbs and dash of salt (according to your taste). Blend well and form small balls of meat mixture. Heat cooking oil in skillet. Brown meat balls evenly (a sprinkle of paprika will hasten browning). Blend yogurt with remainder of onion soup. Mix and chill.

Serve hot meatballs on toothpicks with yogurt dip. (Serves 8)

In the home of ERIC SCOTT *(Ben) the watchword is sweet and sour. Foods with this combination are a favorite with Eric and his two brothers. Of all the delicious foods his mom prepares, Eric's favorite is her sweet and sour stuffed cabbage. This is quite different from Ellen Corby's Danish version.*

Sweet 'n Sour Stuffed Cabbage

1 large firm head cabbage
3 pounds ground chuck beef
1 #2½ can stewed tomatoes
¾ cup raw white rice
1 onion, minced

While the cabbage is cooking in lightly salted boiling water, mix meat, tomatoes and rice until well blended and set aside.

Cook the cabbage until leaves are pliable enough to be removed singly without falling apart. Drain leaves on paper towels. Dice remainder of cabbage and place in the bottom of a large heavy pot along with the onion.

Place ½-1 full teaspoon (depending on size of leaf) of meat mixture on each drained cabbage leaf and roll up. Tie cabbage rolls with string to hold in place. Layer in pot on top of diced cabbage and onion mixture. Cover with water and cook, uncovered, for 30 minutes.

SAUCE
2 10¾-ounce cans tomato soup, undiluted
⅛ teaspoon salt
1 can lemon juice concentrate or 6 ounces freshly squeezed lemon juice
½ cup free-flowing brown sugar

The sweet and sour flavor is very much a personal taste. If the above mixture is too tart, add more sugar. Blend well and pour over the cabbage rolls. Simmer, covered, until done, about 1-1½ hours. (Serves 12)

"I like to cook. It's fun. However, the food I cook myself is usually simple and quite traditional," says RICHARD THOMAS *(John-Boy). "I like all kinds of food though, especially Persian food like chelloke-bab. I love Mexican food, but I don't cook it. I have a friend who cooks a lot of Mexican dishes for me. People do come over to my house and cook for me sometimes, which is nice."*

As a youngster Richard traveled abroad extensively with his parents who danced with such renowned ballet troupes as the Ballet Russe. About the time he was learning to talk, Richard's parents were performing in Havana, Cuba, so it isn't surprising that the first language he learned was Spanish.

Like his television father, RALPH WAITE, *who plays John Walton, Richard is thoroughly enjoying ownership of his very first house. It is a small two-bedroom (one is a study) house that Richard laughingly refers to as Spanish-Tudor because of the combination of English architecture with stucco exterior and "lots of arches." It's where he often entertains on a small scale. Richard's idea of an enjoyable end to a working day is to have two, perhaps three, close friends in to dinner.*

An easy appetizer dip that's tasty and simple enough for a novice to prepare without fear of failure originated in the days of early California. It could very well have provided an entire meal for those early settlers dedicated to preserving the Mexican/Spanish heritage of the state as they worked side by side with the Indians to build the beautiful California missions.

Mexicali Bean Dip

2 cups pinto beans	3 tablespoons chili powder
1 cup chopped onions	1½ teaspoons salt
1 clove garlic, finely chopped	½ cup butter or margarine
1 teaspoon ground cumin seed	½ pound sharp cheddar, grated
3 tablespoons bacon drippings	Dash Mexican hot sauce

Wash beans and soak in water to cover overnight. Transfer beans with water to glass or pyrex pot. Add onions, garlic, cumin seed and bacon drippings. Simmer for 3-4 hours, stirring occasionally to prevent beans from sticking. (If more water must be added at any time use only boiled water, otherwise beans will darken.)

Add chili powder to soft cooked beans and cook over a low flame for 2-3 minutes to allow chili flavor to be absorbed. Remove from fire. Add salt, butter, cheese and hot sauce. Mash beans to smooth consistency, blending with ingredients.

Serve warm with tortilla chips. (Makes 1 quart).

Another favorite of Eric's is his mom's chopped liver appetizer that she serves at holiday dinners.

Chicken Liver Spread

1 pound chicken livers	½ teaspoon freshly
2 tablespoons oil	ground pepper
2 onions, diced	1 teaspoon salt
4 hard-cooked eggs	Parsley

Wash and drain chicken livers thoroughly. In a heavy frying pan heat 1 tablespoon of the oil and brown onion lightly. Add chicken livers and cook for ten minutes.

Place chicken livers, onions and 3 of the eggs in a food grinder, or for a smoother pâté use an electric blender. Remove to bowl and add seasonings and enough of the remaining oil to bind ingredients together for easy spreading.

Mound on a bed of lettuce. Decorate with slices of hard cooked egg yolk and fresh parsley. Chill well before serving with party rye or crackers. (Serves 12)

By his own admission Ralph Waite (John Walton, Sr.), "knows nothing about cooking." But he does have a hearty appetite for good wholesome food and also enjoys more exotic dishes such as raw fish. A hearty appetizer that can do double duty as a meal in itself is what he enjoys most when he's spent a long day in front of the cameras.

As a boy, the eldest of five children, Ralph and his family moved around a lot. His father was an engineer and the family lived in a series of rented homes and apartments throughout Ralph's youth. Today he is the very proud owner of his first house. He's enjoying every moment he can spend there even though he isn't one to putter around in the kitchen.

A tasty antipasto is not only easy to prepare ahead of time, but for Ralph it's often enough to satisfy his hunger at the end of the day. It's also a great way to whet the appetites of guests or family when you're serving an Italian dinner.

Antipasto Special

2 small cans anchovies
2 cans sardines
2 jars marinated artichoke hearts
1 medium-sized can pitted black olives
½ pound Italian salami
½ pound Provolone
cheese
½ pound Prosciutto ham
1 pound fresh zucchini, sliced and sprinkled with garlic powder
Boston lettuce
1 bottle Italian dressing

Drain oil from anchovies, sardines and artichokes. Dain juice from olives.

Arrange the ingredients on individual plates or on a large platter on bed of Boston lettuce leaves. Drizzle with dressing.* Cover with plastic wrap and refrigerate for about 2 hours to allow ingredients to blend well with flavor of dressing. (Serves 6)

*Allow about 1 tablespoon per serving

At 16, JUDY NORTON (Mary Ellen) is a very busy young lady. Her mother says that Judy is so busy doing so many things, such as taking guitar and singing lessons, horseback riding and swimming (when the weather is warm enough) with her friends, going to parties and dances, that she doesn't have much time to cook. Not only is Judy doing all of the fun things every teenaged girl wants to do, she's also earning money and winning awards for her fine acting talents.

Judy lives in the San Fernando Valley with her mom, a very attractive former performer in English music halls, and her younger brother (her parents are divorced). Her sister Ricky, who is two years older than Judy, recently moved into her own apartment. The sisters have always been very close and it was Ricky who first interested Judy in learning to cook. The two girls would spend a lot of time in the kitchen practicing what Ricky learned in her home economics class at high school.

A native Californian, born in Santa Monica, Judy loves Mexican foods. A cooking specialty she loves to prepare and serve to friends on weekends is a taco that is a perfect appetizer anyone can serve to guests no matter what the occasion.

Judy's Taco Treats

10 large tortilla shells
½ cup chopped onion
 2 pounds ground round steak
Salt, pepper and taco sauce to taste
 1 tablespoon salad oil

Heat small amount of cooking or olive oil in a skillet. Lightly brown tortilla shells on one side. Drain well on paper towels. Set aside while preparing the filling.

Sauté onions in small amount of cooking oil until golden in color. Add meat. Season with pepper and salt. Continue browning until meat is well browned. Add taco sauce, a few drops at a time, tasting until desired *hotness* is achieved.

Mix carefully through meat and continue browning over a low flame for a few minutes more to allow sauce to blend through, stirring with wooden spoon to prevent burning.

Drain off fat by piling meat into a colander.

Fill taco shell (fill on side that has been browned) with meat mixture and fold over sandwich style. Fry tacos lightly, turning once so they are golden brown all over. Drain well.

On separate platter arrange avocado chunks, shredded lettuce, tomato slices and and grated Cheddar cheese. Guests can add any or all of these to tacos as desired. (Serves 10)

2

Homemade Breads, Rolls and Biscuits

"Bread is the staff of life."

Nothing is more deep-down soul satisfying than the aroma of freshly baked bread. It immediately conjures up the image of Home. Today, as more and more people are turning back to the simple pleasures of life and to the enjoyment of hearth and home, the art of home bread baking has been revived. The heady fragrances of homemade breads and biscuits are once more filling our country's kitchens.

During the days of the Great Depression when Earl Hamner, Jr., creator of "The Waltons," was growing up in Nelson County, Virginia, his mother did all of her cooking and baking on a wooden stove. Today she fondly reminisces that a wooden stove is still best although she owns a very up-to-date electric range for making biscuits and cakes.

Baking is a very important part of providing good

14

wholesome food for the McDonough family. MARY
ELIZABETH *(Erin), her sister and two brothers have
hearty appetites. Mary is very domestic. She does
needlepoint and crochets and is very into nutrition,
so cooking or baking from scratch, as her mother
usually does for their family of six, is the way Mary
is learning to make her favorite homemade biscuits
and breads. So far she's catching on quite nicely.*

Easy Baking Powder Biscuits

2½ teaspoons baking powder
  2 cups sifted all-purpose flour
 ¾ teaspoon salt
  5 tablespoons shortening
 ¾ cup milk

In a medium-sized bowl add baking powder to
carefully measured flour. Add salt and sift again
into another bowl. Cut in shortening. Add milk
slowly while stirring with a fork. Continue to stir
until a soft dough is formed. This takes about 20
strokes of the fork.

Lightly flour a bread board and turn soft biscuit
dough onto it. Knead dough on board turning about
20 times. To form biscuits pat or roll dough, using
a light touch, to a half-inch thickness. Lightly flour
a biscuit cutter to prevent sticking and cut dough
into 2-inch rounds. Bake on an ungreased cookie
sheet in a preheated 450° oven for 12 to 15 minutes. You will have a good baker's dozen deliciously
fragrant, mouth-watering biscuits that will dress up
any meal.

Fresh Cornbread

1 cup cornmeal	1 teaspoon salt
1 cup sifted flour	1 egg, unbeaten
½ cup sugar	1 cup milk

1 cup melted shortening

In a medium-sized bowl combine the dry ingredients. Add egg, milk and shortening. Stir lightly. Pour into well greased 9-inch loaf pan. Bake in a preheated 425° oven for 20-25 minutes. (Makes 1 loaf)

Mary Elizabeth thinks this is really super with stew or as a snack with fresh butter and a glass of cold milk.

A man-sized sandwich made with freshly baked old-fashioned rye bread is a "meal" Ralph Waite really enjoys. If you want to please the man in your household and have a great time in the preparation try this recipe for rye bread.

Rye Bread

1 package yeast	1½ tablespoons shortening
¼ cup lukewarm water	
1¼ cups scalded milk	1 tablespoon caraway seeds
1½ tablespoons brown sugar	3¾ cups unsifted rye flour
1 tablespoon salt	

1 egg white (optional)

In a small bowl dissolve yeast in lukewarm water and set aside. Combine milk, sugar, salt, shortening and caraway seeds. Cool until lukewarm and add yeast.

Set aside ½ cup flour to use on kneading board. Gradually add remaining rye flour to yeast mixture, stirring to make dough workable. Turn onto a lightly floured board and using reserved flour begin to knead dough until all of the flour is worked in. Do not overmix as this will make the dough sticky.

Grease a large baking pan (round or loaf shaped) and shape dough accordingly. Set loaf into pan, cover with a damp cloth and set in a warm place to rise.

When loaf has doubled in bulk, bake in a pre-heated 375° oven for 50-60 minutes. For an extra touch brush unbeaten egg white across top of loaf before baking. This will produce a shiny glaze and added crunch to the crust.

Allow bread to cool slightly for ease in cutting even though your family will be clamoring for it as soon as it comes out of the oven.

Judy Norton's mother and grandparents are from England. Jon Walmsley was born there also, so the two have a common family heritage. A favorite for tea time or at supper in England is what we call Boston Brown Bread.

The traditional way to make Boston Brown Bread is to steam it in a mold. But this is a simpler method and the result is just as tasty.

Boston Brown Bread

2 teaspoons soda
2 cups dark raisins
2 tablespoons sweet butter
2 cups brown sugar
2 eggs, slightly beaten
1 teaspoon salt

2 cups all-purpose flour
2 cups whole-wheat flour
2 teaspoons vanilla
1 cup chopped walnuts
  (optional)

Add soda and raisins to 2 cups boiling water. Mix and set aside to cool. Cream butter with sugar, add eggs, sifted flour, salt. Alternately mix flour with raisin mixture, small amounts at a time, blending with spatula or wooden spoon. Add vanilla. Add walnuts if desired.

The English version is baked in gold-lined tins (6 tin cans). They are half filled and baked in a preheated 350° oven for about 50 minutes.

But don't despair if you haven't any gold-lined tins on hand. A 10 x 6 x 2 inch loaf pan, lightly greased, will do nicely. You should bake for about 1 hour at 350°, then test with a toothpick to make certain it is done as it takes longer in a loaf pan.

Remove from oven and allow to stand in the pan for 10 minutes, then remove from pan and let cool on a wire rack.

You may want to try Judy's suggestion of baking the dough in paper-lined muffin tins filled halfway for individual Boston Brown Bread servings. Bake at 400° for 25 minutes. Makes about 3 dozen. They are delicious with frankfurter dishes and boiled beef dinners or spread with cream cheese topping as a tasty and nutritious midday snack.

Nearly all of the cast of "The Waltons," especially Mary, Ellen Corby, Will Geer and Jon Walmsley, are health conscious. They are really tuned into natural foods and are especially fond of sandwiches made of whole-grained flours, such as whole-wheat.

Whole-Wheat Bread Treat

1 cup milk	¼ cup lukewarm water
½ tablespoon butter	2 cups whole-wheat flour
½ teaspoon salt	¾ cup soy flour or carob
¼ cup natural honey	powder
1 package yeast	

Heat milk, stir in butter, salt and honey. Set aside to cool to lukewarm. Dissolve yeast in warm water and add to milk mixture in a large bowl. Using low speed of electric mixer beat in whole-wheat flour. Add soy flour or carob powder and stir to blend ingredients thoroughly.

Flour a board or table and turn dough onto it. Begin kneading, adding only enough whole-wheat flour to make dough smooth and pliable. Set dough in a large pyrex bowl that has been well greased. Cover with a clean cloth or towel and set in warm place (about 85°) for 1 hour. (The inside of your oven is usually warm enough, even if it isn't turned on, to use as a warming place for the bread dough.)

Punch down to original size and let rise again. Grease a loaf pan (8x4 inches) and set dough in pan to rise with towel covering it. When dough has risen to top of pan remove towel and bake in a preheated 375° oven for 45 minutes. Remove from pan and let cool on wire rack. (Makes 1 loaf)

If you prefer a round bread use a round baking pan. For added good taste that Mary loves mix a small amount of finely crushed fresh berries with the honey. If the berries are tart increase the amount of honey accordingly.

In the Scott household bagels for Sunday break-fast are a real favorite. Eric likes his toasted, spread with whipped cream cheese and topped with a slice of smoked salmon and tomato. Sometimes he makes a snack of a fresh bagel with butter and jam.

The fun of baking bagels is in using your imagi-nation. Simply by adding variations to the dough such as grated Cheddar cheese, cooked onion bits or garlic powder; by substituting whole-wheat flour for the all-purpose flour called for in the recipe; or by adding raisins, or herbs (Will Geer's favorite addi-tion to enhance just about anything is fresh herbs) you can create your own bagel masterpieces.

Basic Bagels

    2 packages yeast
4½ cups sifted all-purpose flour
1½ cups lukewarm water
    3 tablespoons sugar
    1 tablespoon salt (or garlic salt if you like the flavor)

Combine yeast and 1¾ cups flour in a large bowl. In a smaller bowl mix together water, sugar and salt. Add to yeast/flour mixture. Beat on low speed of electric mixer for about ½ minute, being careful to scrape sides of bowl with rubber spatula so all of flour is well blended. Beat for additional 3 minutes on high speed. (Add variations at this stage if you desire.)

By hand stir in enough of remaining flour to make a dough of medium stiff consistency. Knead on lightly floured board until dough is smooth and shiny. Cover with a clean cloth and let rise for about 15 minutes.

Cut dough into 12 parts. Shape into smooth balls. With your forefinger well floured punch a hole through the center of each dough ball. Shape hole with finger and form dough into the shape of a bagel. Let rise, covered, for about 20 minutes.

In a heavy pot bring 1 gallon of water and 1 tablespoon of sugar to a boil. Reduce to simmer and begin dropping bagels into simmering water three at a time. Cook, turning just once with tongs (gently), about 5 minutes.

Drain cooked bagels on paper towels. Set on an ungreased cookie sheet and bake for 30-35 minutes at 375°, or until golden in color. (Makes 12 bagels)

Attending to the needs of her family was a chore of love for tiny, red-haired Doris Hamner. In the days of the Big Depression such things as automatic washing machines and dryers were unheard of, and she had plenty to do taking care of a five room, two-story house and eight children. But even so Mrs. Hamner enjoyed preparing special treats for her husband and children to enjoy at supper, a time for much lively discussion.

"Sometimes my mother would make Parkerhouse rolls," Earl Jr. recalls. "I remember coming home from school and the dough would be rising in pans all around the kitchen. I could smell the yeast."

Plain Yeast Roll Dough

1 cake yeast	1 teaspoon salt
½ cup lukewarm water	1 egg, well beaten
¼ cup plus 1 teaspoon sugar	3½ cups sifted all-purpose flour
1 cup milk, scalded and cooled to lukewarm	¾ cup melted shortening, cooled

In a warm bowl crumble compressed cake yeast in water to which 1 teaspoon sugar has been added. Stir to dissolve. In a separate bowl combine milk, salt and ¼ cup sugar. (It is very important that all the liquids be lukewarm as anything warmer stops the action of the yeast.)

Mix yeast with milk, add egg and beat as hard as you can until ingredients are well blended. Add 1½ cups flour gradually, beating well until mixture is smooth. Add shortening and beat again. Set aside about 2 tablespoons flour and gradually add remainder to mixture in bowl until a soft dough is formed. Continue mixing until dough is smooth in texture.

Lightly flour a board or table and turn out dough. Let stand for a few minutes before starting to knead. Flour hands well and begin kneading gently, punching down and folding over until dough is smooth and elastic with a shiny surface and no trace of stickiness is left. This may take 10-15 minutes. Use the reserved 2 tablespoons flour to help shape dough into a smooth satiny ball.

Set in a large greased bowl (turning once so surface is well greased), place in warm spot and cover with towel or wax paper. Let rise until double in bulk (1½-2 hours).

Turn dough out on floured board again and shape into:

Parkerhouse Rolls

Roll dough out to a 1/3-inch thickness. Using a floured round cookie or biscuit cutter begin to cut out rolls. Melt ½-1 cup butter to brush tops. Using the handle of a knife make a crease across each roll just off center. Brush surface with melted butter and fold larger end of each round over smaller one, shaping into ovals. Pinch edges so rolls are sealed well.

Place rolls on a lightly greased cookie sheet about 1 inch apart. Brush tops with additional melted butter. Cover and let rise again until double in bulk, about 30 minutes. Bake for 15-20 minutes at 375°. (Makes about 3 dozen rolls)

This basic dough recipe can be used to prepare tasty and healthful Cheese Crescents, great with salads, soups or just for snacking.

Cheese Crescents

Roll dough out to a half-inch thickness and cut into triangular pieces. Brush inside of each triangle with melted butter. Sprinkle with grated Cheddar cheese. Starting at the wide end of each triangle begin to roll up dough. Brush surface of each roll with unbeaten egg white and set on a lightly greased cookie sheet. Cover and let rise. Brush surface of each Crescent with unbeaten egg white. Bake 10–15 minutes or until golden brown in a preheated 350° oven. (Makes about 4 dozen Crescents)

3

Casseroles/
Budget/One-Dish Meals

*"The chief pleasure in eating does not
consist in costly seasonings or exquisite
flavor, but in yourself." Horace*

---

*Nothing says "you" as much as a casserole. Not
only are they an economical way to stretch an ailing
food budget, but they allow you, as the cook, to be
creative and let your imagination soar. You can
add to the basic ingredients of any casserole or one-
dish meal as your creativity allows.*

*The depression of "The Waltons" took place some
forty years ago, but these days with food prices
continuing to soar everyone is trying to find ways
to prepare tasty meals without overstraining their
wallets. Cast members of "The Waltons" are as
aware of the economic pinch today as the real Waltons were back in the 1930's.*

*Casserole dishes can be dressed up to serve to
guests for the most gala of dinner parties. They are*

nutritious and may be prepared ahead of time to be stored in refrigerator or freezer until needed. Anything that saves time is welcomed by the cast members as well as the mothers of the "Walton" children, most of whom spend their days on the set since the law requires a child actor (under 18) to be accompanied by an adult. Those mothers who hire a sit in, such as Kami Cotler's mother, do so because they have important full-time jobs elsewhere.

A popular accompaniment to broiled chicken is one that Judy Norton's mom prepares.

California Barley Casserole

2 tablespoons butter or margarine
1 cup pearl barley
1 tablespoon chopped fresh parsley
1 can onion soup plus 1 can water
1 beef bouillon cube
1 4-ounce can mushrooms, undrained

Melt butter and add barley. Cook, stirring often, until lightly toasted. Add parsley, soup, water, bouillon cube and mushrooms with liquid. Bring to a slow boil. Turn into a buttered 1½-quart covered casserole and bake in a preheated 350° oven for 1 hour. (Serves 5)

Judy often has friends dropping by on weekends when she's not working at the studio. A favorite one-dish meal that's easy to put together and tastes great is:

Nippy Hamburger In A Dish

  1 tablespoon cooking oil
2½ pounds ground chuck or round steak
  1 onion, chopped or diced
  1 6-ounce package wide noodles
  ½ jar of melted cheese spread (on the sharp side)-4 oz.
Paprika

Heat the oil in a heavy skillet. Brown meat with onion. While meat is browning cook noodles in boiling salted water according to package directions.

Add cheese and soup to meat mixture and stir through with wooden spoon. Continue cooking over a low flame for about 2–3 minutes more.

Drain noodles in a colander. Lightly butter a 2-quart casserole dish and alternately layer noodles and meat mixture in dish; first and last layer should be noodles. Sprinkle lightly with paprika.

Bake in a preheated 300° oven for about 20-25 minutes, or pile cooked noodles onto a platter and spoon meat mixture over them for a fast cook-and-serve meal. Serve with crusty French bread and a green salad with your favorite dressing. (Serves 6-8)

One evening when Judy, her mom and Ricky were in the mood for Mexican food but didn't want to go out to eat they put their imaginations together and concocted a dish that even Judy's brother proclaimed as "neat."

Meatballs Olé

2 pounds ground lean beef	1 8-ounce can tomato sauce plus 1 can cold water
Garlic salt to taste	
1 tablespoon cooking oil	1 4-ounce can green chili peppers
½ cup chopped onions	
1 8-ounce can red kidney beans, drained	Dash hot sauce (optional)

Season ground meat with garlic salt to taste. Shape into miniature meatballs. Heat cooking oil in a frying pan and lightly fry meatballs until brown. Add onions and brown.

Remove to a 2-quart casserole dish. Mix kidney beans, tomato sauce and water in small bowl. Add to meatballs. Cut up chili peppers and lay across meatball mixture in casserole. Cook in a slow oven (or simmer on top of stove) until meatballs are thoroughly cooked and sauce is well blended.

Serve over bed of rice that is slightly on the dry side so sauce will not make it soggy. (Serves 8)

A fresh fruit salad with lime sherbet is how Judy likes to round out this easy to prepare meal.

Ellen Corby's favorite hobby is traveling. "If I wasn't an actress what I'd like to do most is travel and write," she says.

These days Ellen is doing all three and enjoying every bit of the time she spends at her work and her hobby. At 60+ years of age she has a zest for life that many of the youngsters on the show not only admire but also hope to emulate "when they grow up." After forty years in the business, Ellen's por-

trayal of the crusty grandmother with the heart of gold has earned her deep affection in the hearts of fans all over the country and even abroad. Her face has always been familiar to movie fans since she has played major supporting roles in about 300 films. Among the most memorable are I Remember Mama, Little Women *and* Shane.

It's the role of Grandma Walton that has made Ellen a household name. She has become a superstar at an age when most women would be content to sit in their rockers and dwell on their memories. Ellen Corby is filled with vitality and her interests include the practice of yoga to keep her body agile (she can bend over and touch her toes with graceful ease), but it is travel that holds real fascination for her.

Growing up in the restaurant business has given Ellen a keen appreciation of good cooking. Although she puts Danish cooking first on her list of preferences, Ellen is also fond of French and Italian food.

Parmesan Chicken Breasts

2 chicken breasts, boned and split
Garlic salt
Dash each oregano and marjoram
¼ cup grated Parmesan cheese
1 cup very fine cracker crumbs
½ cup melted butter

Wash and dry chicken breasts. Sprinkle lightly with garlic salt. Add seasonings and grated cheese to cracker crumbs. Dip chicken first in melted butter, then in cracker crumbs. Set chicken in a buttered shallow baking dish. Drizzle with remaining butter and crumb/cheese mixture and bake for 1 hour in a preheated 350° oven. (Serves 4)

One of Ellen's favorite blue plate specials *on the menu of her mother's restaurant was another dish made with forcemeat. It was, and still is, an economical meal and one that Ellen's brother and father were equally fond of for dinner.*

Frikadeller

Form large balls of forcemeat (see recipe on page 3). Fry in a generous amount of sweet butter over a low flame in heavy frying pan. Stir now and then to prevent burning. Serve with thick slices of pumpernickel bread and butter with Danish pastry for dessert. (Serves 4–6)

Since her turn on to natural foods Ellen enjoys all kinds of vegetables. Back in the restaurant days frikadeller was served with steamed vegetables such as carrots, cabbage or string beans. Today you might want to add zucchini (her favorite), eggplant, broccoli, cauliflower or summer squash.

"I must make my sweet and sour meat loaf at least three times a month," says Eric Scott's mom. "It's a big favorite with all three of our boys and it's certainly economical."

Sweet and Sour Meat Loaf

1 8-ounce can tomato sauce	1 egg, slightly beaten
¼ cup brown sugar, firmly packed	1 small onion, minced
	¼ cup crushed crackers
¼ cup vinegar	2 pounds ground chuck steak
1 teaspoon prepared mustard	Salt and pepper to taste

In a large bowl mix tomato sauce with sugar, vinegar and mustard, stirring until sugar is completely dissolved. Mix egg, onion, cracker crumbs and meat. Season to taste (Mr. Scott recently suffered a heart attack so Mrs. Scott uses a salt substitute). Add ½ cup tomato sauce mixture to meat mixture and shape into oval loaf. Turn into 1½-quart shallow baking dish.

Pour remaining tomato sauce over meat loaf and bake for 1 hour in a preheated 350° oven. Baste with sauce occasionally. (Serves 8)

Baked potatoes, "Get It All Together" salad (see recipe on page 45) and a steamed green vegetable accompany this family favorite.

Eric is learning how to cook and he's a very imaginative chef judging by the Saturday morning breakfast he puts together. All of the Scott boys learned to cook at a very early age by hanging around the kitchen and asking their mom questions. Eric's older brother took a senior cooking course at school and he's been giving Eric some pointers, too. Mr. Scott is also handy around the kitchen stove, so the entire Scott family (even the 10 year old) are self-sufficient in the area of meal preparation. They all enjoy doing their own thing with food. Eric's breakfast specialty was copied from something he's watched his dad cook many times.

Eric's Special Denver Omelet

Beat 2 eggs, adding a few drops of water, and set aside. Cut up or dice the following: onion, green pepper, salami, bologna, mushrooms, tomatoes. . . . anything else that appeals to your taste buds and happens to be in the refrigerator. Heat 1 tablespoon butter in a frying pan and sauté all ingredients but the eggs. Drain on a paper towel and melt an additional tablespoon butter in pan. Pour in eggs and cook until edges start to turn golden and center is beginning to bubble or puff. Add onion mixture and fold omelet in half. Continue cooking until eggs are done to your taste. (Serves 1)

In the Scott home dinner is a lively meal, much as it is on "The Waltons," except that it's the three boys who do most of the talking. "The boys usually discuss school happenings or Eric may tell us about something that happened at the studio. My husband and I don't usually say much except to answer any of their questions," Mrs. Scott relates.

Dreaming up man-pleasing meals is a source of real pride and pleasure to her. On the set of "The Waltons" there's a great deal of recipe exchanging among the mothers of the Walton "kids." One that Judy Scott thinks is excellent as a company casserole is:

Casserole BBQ Chicken

1 3-to 3½-pound chicken, cut up	1 cup catsup
½ cup flour	1 cup water
2 teaspoons salt	2 tablespoons brown sugar
½ cup salad oil	2 tablespoons Worcestershire sauce
1 medium onion, sliced	
½ cup chopped celery	Dash pepper
¼ cup minced ground pepper	

Dip chicken pieces in flour that has been mixed with salt. Fry in hot oil until golden brown. Remove chicken to a 3-quart casserole. If desired, pour into casserole along with chicken all but 2 tablespoons of fat from the skillet (to keep chicken from drying out).

Add onion to fat remaining in skillet and sauté until golden and tender. Add celery, green pepper, catsup, water, sugar and seasonings. Mix well and pour over chicken. Refrigerate, covered, for 1-2 hours.

Bake chicken, covered, in a preheated 350° oven for 1 hour and 45 minutes, or until tender. (Be sure to use a casserole dish that can go from refrigerator to oven.) (Serves 4)

Another economical and tasty one-dish meal that Mrs. Scott prepares often for her family is one that Eric is learning how to make himself.

Beef and Rice Budget Dinner

1 5-ounce package pre-cooked rice (or 1⅓ cups)	1 pound ground chuck beef
	1 teaspoon salt
2 tablespoons butter or margarine	Dash pepper
1½ cups diced celery	1 10¾-ounce can condensed tomato soup, undiluted
2 tablespoons minced onions	¼ cup cold water

Cook rice according to package directions. While rice is cooking melt butter in a skillet. Sauté celery and onions until tender.

Drain rice thoroughly and place in a lightly greased 1½-quart casserole. Top with celery mixture. In a bowl season meat with salt and pepper and brown in butter remaining in skillet. Add to celery mixture in casserole.

Combine soup with water and pour over meat. Bake for 35 minutes in a preheated 375° oven. (Serves 6)

Although he has lived in this country since infancy Jon Walmsley is partial to English cooking. Before the family moved to Los Angeles they lived in San Diego and were very active in the British Club where people from all over England who had moved to the U.S. met on a regular basis for social gatherings. Pot luck dinners were one of frequently planned get-togethers. Mrs. Walmsley often prepared her special Steak and Kidney Pie, a British favorite.

Steak and Kidney Pie

Puff pastry or prepared
    pie crust mix
1 tablespoon flour
¼ teaspoon salt
¼ teaspoon freshly
    ground pepper
1½ pounds round steak,
    cut into 1-inch cubes

2 tablespoons butter
½ pound beef kidney,
    carefully trimmed
1 medium onion,
    chopped
1 cup beef stock or
    water

Prepare the pie crust and set aside. Mix the flour with salt and pepper and dredge the steak pieces thoroughly. In a Dutch oven melt the butter and brown the meat on all sides. Add the onion and sauté for 5 minutes. Add the beef stock and simmer, covered, for 1 to 1½ hours until meat is tender. Add the kidney pieces during the last half hour of simmering. Thicken the broth with flour which has been blended with cold water, allowing 1½ teaspoons of flour for each cup of broth. Transfer the mixture to a pie dish and cover with the pie crust. Make a small hole in the center of the crust to allow for the escape of steam and brush with milk. Bake in a preheated 450° oven for 30 minutes. (Serves 4-6).

4

Soups

"A hearty soup is a meal in itself."

Meat rationing and victory gardens stand out in Ralph Waite's memories of his teen years. He often thinks of the similarity between his own family and the Waltons. With two sisters and two brothers younger than himself dinnertime was anything but dull. "We had a lot of energy going, there was a lot of talking at the table," he remembers fondly.

His mother, a good cook, had to provide nutritious, inexpensive and tasty meals to please her growing children and hard-working husband. Soup was frequently on the menu because it was easy to cook up a pot of good soup without using up valuable meat coupons and still please the family. A good pea soup with vegetables was almost a meal in itself.

Cousin Carole's Split Pea Soup

1 8-ounce package split peas	3 tablespoons salt (or to taste)
1 4-ounce package fine barley	A meaty ham bone, 1 pound short ribs or 1 pound shank meat
1 onion	
3 small carrots, finely chopped	3⅓ quarts cold water

Add all the ingredients to the water in heavy soup kettle, partially cover and cook over a high flame for 20 minutes. Remove cover and skim off excess fat from water with wooden spoon.

Again partially cover (allow lid to sit lopsided so pot is not completely covered) and cook over a medium flame for 45 minutes. Stir ingredients through now and then to prevent sticking. Cover tightly and simmer for 1 hour. Remove and discard onion.

This soup tastes best if allowed to stand and thicken for at least an hour before serving. Stir through and reheat on a very low flame. (Serves 6)

If desired, other vegetables such as cauliflower or okra may be added during last hour of cooking.

In the McDonough household soup is served often. A rich source of vitamin C and protein, as well as Mary Elizabeth's favorite, is her mother's:

Fresh Cream of Tomato Soup

2 vegetable bouillon cubes	2 tablespoons sweet butter
2 cups boiling water	3 tablespoons flour
3-4 medium-sized soft tomatoes, peeled and diced	3 cups cold milk
	1 teaspoon salt (or to taste)

In a small pot dissolve bouillon cubes in boiling water. Add tomatoes and simmer, uncovered, until tomatoes are mushy. Remove from fire. Put cooked tomatoes (retain liquid) through a fine strainer and mash as finely as possible, letting whatever comes through strainer accumulate in a small bowl. Return mashed tomatoes to liquid and set aside.

Melt butter in top of double boiler over direct flame, but do not let butter burn. Slowly add flour, mixing and blending well. Stir in milk slowly to avoid lumps. Add salt and tomatoes. Cook over boiling water in top of double boiler until thickened to serving consistency. (Makes about 6 soup cup servings)

"We were not a farm family. That's a misconception many people have gotten from the show," says Earl Hamner, Jr., who patterned "The Waltons" after his own family. "My father was a woodsman and he sold lumber and firewood. But living in the country, and with such a large family (there were eight children in the real *Waltons), we did have a vegetable garden." A big field of corn enabled his mother to produce a number of simple but hearty dishes that provided good nutrition for her hard-working husband and growing children.*

The family shared all three meals together, even lunch. Since they lived close to the school they would all arrive filled with news of the morning's events and hungry for whatever their mother had prepared. The meals were plain, but good, and as Earl recalls, "My mother made fresh hot biscuits for every meal." Soup and hot biscuits was often enough of a lunch to send them back to finish the school day feeling well fed. On specially blustery winter days a hearty corn chowder was appreciated.

Mrs. Hamner's Special Corn Chowder

1 onion, sliced
4 ounces salt pork, diced
4 cups fresh corn, cut
   from the cob
8 cups hot water
2 cups cream

6 tablespoons sweet
   butter
4 teaspoons salt
Freshly ground black
   pepper (optional)

In a large heavy soup kettle sauté onion with salt pork. When onion is tender add corn and water. Cover and simmer for about 10 minutes. Add cream, butter and salt. If desired, small amounts of pepper may be added. Continue cooking until corn is tender (Serves 8-10)

Another soup that Mrs. Hamner cooked often for her brood during the cold weather was:

Bean Soup

2 cups dried beans (black, lima or navy)	1 medium onion, chopped
½-1 pound ham, cut into chunks	2 celery stalks, chopped
½ cup sliced carrots	Salt to taste

Soak beans overnight in cold water. In the morning, or when ready to cook soup, drain off water. Fill a large kettle with 14 cups water and add beans and ham. Cover and bring to a boil. Reduce heat to simmer and cook for about 3 hours. Add carrots, onions and celery. Salt to taste (if ham is salty enough soup may not need extra salt). Cover again and simmer for an additional 30 minutes. (Serves 8-10)

Like Earl Hamner, Jr., creator of "The Waltons," Will Geer grew up in a small town. It was as a boy in the farming town of Frankfort, Indiana, that Grandpa Walton learned to love and respect the bountiful harvest provided by Mother Nature. The outdoors and what the earth supplies in the way of beauty and food is what turns on this eminent actor. After a half century of performing in just about every phase of the entertainment business Will Geer remains at heart a country boy.

His home today, one of a complex of chalet apartments he owns in Hollywood, is surrounded by a garden planted and tended with loving care. He is happiest living close to nature despite world-wide acclaim for his superb talents as an actor. A meal for Will Geer is incomplete without a vegetable

*freshly picked from his flourishing garden. Soup
prepared with vegetables from the garden has a taste
that cannot be equaled.*

*A favorite with the Hamner family, the McDon-
oughs and Grandpa Walton is:*

Old Fashioned Vegetable Soup

2 meaty soup bones
1 pound lean short ribs
 of beef or chicken
 breasts
3 quarts cold water
2-3 teaspoons salt
4 tomatoes, diced or
 cubed
5 white potatoes, peeled
 and cubed
½ cup fresh green beans
¼ cup sliced celery

1 cup fresh corn, cut
 from the cob
1 large onion, chopped
4 medium carrots, sliced
Dash freshly ground pep-
 per (optional)
½ teaspoon thyme
 (optional)
½ cup fresh green peas
2 pounds zucchini, sliced
 in half-inch pieces

Place soup bones and meat or chicken in a large
kettle with water. Bring to a boil. Skim off fat and
foam and reduce flame. Add 2 teaspoons salt, tomatoes, potatoes, green beans and celery. Simmer
for about 15 minutes. Add corn, onions, carrots and
seasonings (taste before adding more salt) and
simmer for about 45 minutes. Add green peas and
zucchini and any other quick cooking vegetable
such as spinach or mushrooms and simmer an additional 15 minutes, or until meat and all vegetables
are tender.

Remove soup bones and meat, set aside. Stir
through soup before serving piping hot. (Serves
about 12)

*Another soup favorite of the Hamner family and
one Eric Scott lists on his menu of favorite holiday
dishes is chicken soup. In the days of the depression people who lived in the country raised chickens
for the eggs and for food, Earl Hamner remembers.*

Traditional Chicken Soup

1 3-pound chicken, cut in quarters

4 quarts water

1 large onion, peeled

1 tablespoon salt

2 carrots, scraped and cut into chunks

2 large stalks celery, cut up

1 parsnip

small bunch fresh parsley

Clean the chicken parts including the neck. (Giblets may be frozen for use later in gravy, or stuffing.
Freeze chicken liver separately until you have
enough to make chopped liver spread or pâté.) Fill
a deep kettle with water and add onion. Bring to a
slow boil and add chicken. Lower heat and continue
cooking for about 1 hour. Skim off foam from top of
water while cooking. Add salt. Simmer for 30 minutes longer. Add carrots, celery and parsnip. Cook
15 minutes then add parsley and continue cooking
until chicken is tender. Entire cooking time takes
about 2 hours.

Remove celery, parsnip, parsley and onion from
soup. Let stand for 5 minutes then remove chicken
to platter (delicious served cold or use in croquettes
or chicken salad). Skim off fat from surface of soup.

Makes about 2 quarts of chicken broth that may
be served with crackers, hot biscuits, rice, noodles
or matzo balls, as desired.

MICHAEL LEARNED *(Olivia Walton) learned to prepare a number of French dishes from her former
mother-in-law. Although she loves to cook, and
does so whenever she has the time, Miss Learned
has a housekeeper who takes care of the domestic
chores that her time-consuming career doesn't allow her to do. Her three sons Caleb 19, Chris 16,
and Lucas 11 get all of her attention when she goes
home after a busy day at the studio.*

*This favorite onion soup, one associated with the
finest of French chefs and served throughout France,
is simple to prepare and can be served elegantly
enough to please the most finicky eater.*

French Onion Soup

4 tablespoons sweet
butter
8 small onions, finely
sliced
6 cups chicken soup*
or bouillon
1-1½ cups dry white wine

Salt and pepper to taste
Homemade croutons (see
below) or toasted slices of
French bread
½ cup grated Parmesan
cheese

In a heavy soup pot melt butter and slowly sauté
the onions until golden in color. Add soup and
wine. Season to taste and bring to a boil over
medium heat. Simmer, covered, until onions are
soft, about 30 minutes.

Serve piping hot in individual soup cups. For
garnish float croutons or a slice of toast in each
cup. Sprinkle with grated cheese. (Serves 6)

---

* This is a great way to make use of any leftover chicken soup,
which you've wisely put away in your freezer for just such an occasion.

HOMEMADE CROUTONS

Remove the crusts from 6 slices of white bread, cut into cubes and dry in a very slow oven (275°) until crisp and lightly browned. Sprinkle with herbs before putting in oven for a zestier flavor. Homemade croutons are also good in salads.

Miss Learned's father worked for the State Department while she was growing up so the family did a great deal of traveling. Born in Washington, D.C., Michael moved from there to New England where she discovered the special taste of genuine Yankee cooking.

Easy Fish Chowder

¼ cup butter
¼ cup onion chopped
1 8-ounce can clams
½ pound cod fillet, cut into chunks
½ pound cooked baby shrimp
1 4-ounce can oysters
3 tablespoons all-purpose flour
2 cups diced raw potatoes
4½ cups milk
1 cup light cream
½-1 teaspoon salt
Dash white pepper
4 ounces Cheddar cheese

Melt butter in heavy saucepan. Sauté onion until just soft. Gradually stir in flour and seasonings. Remove from heat. Add 1½ cups milk and ½ cup cream. Stir well. Add potatoes, cover and return saucepan to stove. Cook over medium heat for 10 minutes. Add remaining milk and cream. Cook additional 10 minutes, or until potatoes are just about done. Stir in cheese, fish and shell fish. Heat to boiling on low flame, stirring now and then. (Serves 6-8)

5
Salads

In California salads are very popular. A salad often serves as an entire meal for members of the Walton family, especially if it includes protein in the form of fish, cheese, turkey or chicken. In the Scott household a big salad served with dinner is Mrs. Scott's way of getting Eric to eat vegetables. The Walmsley's have been watching their diet and eating a lot of salads to help them stick to it. Richard Thomas includes a salad as a basic part of his favorite home-cooked dinners. He prefers his own, specially mixed salad dressing. In the McDonough home Mary's favorite salad is one she tosses together with a lot of good things from the health food store. Will Geer, our nature lover, describes a salad so beautifully it equals that of an artist painting a portrait, with a touch of humor for good measure.

Will Geer likes raw vegetables almost as much as he likes actors. Both are very colorful and mix well at parties, although he finds some actors harder to digest. His garden is just full of young carrots, beets, turnips and radishes waiting for that special party to be discovered.

Will Geer's Raw Vegetable Salad

carrots
beets
turnips
radishes

Wash the raw vegetables carefully, being sure not to remove any make-up (just dirt). Next, put them through the finest cone of a grater to make long threads. Dress a serving plate with a bronze lettuce leaf (producer-type) and pile one mound of each vegetable in a triangle (being certain to get the carrots' good side) and in the center place the radishes.

Pass a bowl of sour cream dressing that is slightly tinted green by the addition of a few drops of food color (this is to impress the Hollywood types at your table).

Eric Scott's Get It All Together Salad

1 bunch raw spinach, torn into bite-sized pieces
2 medium zucchini, sliced
1 small cauliflower, cut up in small chunks
½ pound mushrooms, sliced
alfalfa sprouts (amount is optional)

Wash spinach carefully to remove sand and dry on paper towels or in a vegetable spinner before tearing. Toss all the ingredients in salad bowl. Chill thoroughly. Serve with bottled Italian dressing. (Serves 6)

Richard's Special Homemade Salad Dressing

¼ cup salad vinegar or wine vinegar
¼ cup water
½ cup salad oil
1 clove garlic, peeled
⅛ teaspoon dry mustard

Pinch oregano, thyme, marjoram and any other fresh herbs on hand
Honey (optional)

Shake well in a cruet and chill thoroughly. Remove garlic, shake again and pour just enough to coat salad greens without saturating them into limpness. Richard says he just throws it all together when he is preparing the dressing and keeps mixing until it tastes the way he likes it. (Yields ¾ cup)

Mary Elizabeth's Health Salad

4 cups torn spinach leaves
4 cups endive, watercress, iceberg lettuce, torn
1 pound bean sprouts

1 avocado, peeled and cubed or cut in thick slices
1 eggplant, sliced
Salt to taste
½ cup sesame or sunflower seeds

Wash spinach and all lettuce thoroughly. Drain well and chill. Just before ready to serve toss all ingredients except the seeds in a bowl. Season to taste with salt. Add your favorite salad dressing, mix well and sprinkle with sesame or sunflower seeds. (Serves 8)

A delicious and different dressing for this salad,

and one in keeping with the health motif, can be made as follows:

Herbed Yogurt Dressing

½ teaspoon oregano
⅛ teaspoon garlic powder
 2 cups unflavored yogurt

Blend herbs into yogurt and chill well before tossing with salad. (Makes 2 cups)

Fresh fruit is a favorite with all the cast members of "The Waltons." Nothing is more refreshing after a morning of working under hot lights in front of the cameras than a luncheon of luscious fruit salad with an equally delightful fruit-flavored dressing. This one is a combination of everyone's favorite fruit salad.

Walton Family—California Fresh Fruit Salad

1½ cups green grapes, stemmed and rinsed well

 2 cups sliced fresh strawberries

 1 cup raspberries, left whole if berries are small

 2 cups cubed canteloupe

 1 cup casaba melon, cubed or sliced

 4 oranges, peeled and sectioned

 1 grapefruit, peeled and sectioned

 4 fresh peaches, peeled and cubed

 1 pineapple, peeled, cored and cubed

 ½ cup chopped pecans and walnuts, mixed

Mint sprigs

Toss all the ingredients lightly in a large bowl and chill for 2 hours (unless fruit has been thoroughly chilled in the refrigerator). Serve on individual salad plates lined with Bibb lettuce. Decorate with mint sprigs. (Serves 8)

Pass a simple dressing of yogurt flavored with orange or pineapple juice and enough honey to sweeten blended in a mixer until smooth.

For a more exotic dressing try the following:

¾ cup mayonnaise
½ cup orange juice
½ teaspoon curry powder

Blend thoroughly and chill before mixing through the salad. (Makes about 1 cup)

Another delicious dressing for fresh fruit salad is made with buttermilk:

¾ cup mayonnaise
½ cup buttermilk
1 tablespoon grated orange peel
1 tablespoon orange juice
Honey (optional)

Blend thoroughly and chill. Add a touch honey, if dressing is too tangy.

When she's working Ellen Corby likes to eat her main meal at noon. So a salad that's filling and nourishing, with a good portion of protein, is what she considers the proper lunch for her. It keeps her going until she gets home.

High Energy Salad

2 hard-cooked eggs,
   peeled and quartered
½ head iceberg lettuce,
   torn in small pieces
½ bunch watercress,
   torn in small pieces
½ head romaine lettuce,
   torn in small pieces
4 slices American
   cheese, cut into strips
2 cooked chicken
   breasts, cubed

6-8 cherry tomatoes,
   halved
2 apples, cored and cut
   into bite-sized chunks
¾ cup Italian or
   Thousand Island
   dressing
Endive
Green pepper strips
   (optional)

Have all ingredients well chilled. Toss together
with the salad dressing of your choice and serve on
bed of endive. Decorate with strips of green pepper
if desired. (Serves 4)

*Nutritious salads were regularly served in her
mother's restaurant with cabbage in one form or another often as the basis. A simple, satisfying and
very nourishing accompaniment to any meat dish
is:*

Apple Slaw

1 tablespoon lemon juice or cider vinegar
½ tablespoon sugar
½ cup sour cream
1 cup unpeeled, cored and chopped red apples
2 cups shredded green and red cabbage (mixed)
Salt and pepper to taste

Blend lemon juice and sugar with sour cream. Toss with the remaining ingredients. Season and refrigerate until well chilled. (Serves 4)

Jon Walmsley has no weight problem. At 5'9" he weighs a very lean 135 pounds, but as a professional actor he is very much aware of what the camera's eye can reveal. So Jon is glad to go along with his mother's diet plan to serve salads often. Getting into the habit of not overeating will pay off, Jon feels, because he won't have to worry about putting on extra pounds that the camera picks up like a magnet. As it is, everyone on the show appears from five to ten pounds heavier than they really are because of some subtle trick of the camera lens.

When salad is served at the Walmsley dinnertable it's always simple, but tasty. Mrs. Walmsley takes pride in providing her son and husband, both hard working men, with meals that supply all of the essential vitamins and minerals they need to keep up their vitality.

Seafood Salad

1 pound cooked and cleaned shrimp (The equivalent of 1 cup)
½ cup crabmeat chunks
½ cup pineapple chunks
Endive or watercress
½ cup low-calorie French dressing, chilled
3 asparagus spears, cooked and chilled

Combine shrimp, crabmeat and pineapple chunks. Refrigerate for 30 minutes to 1 hour. In meantime wash and dry greens. Toss fish mixture with dressing in a small bowl. Serve on individual salad plates on a bed of salad greens. Arrange on asparagus across top of salad for garnish. Serve with crackers and wheat thins. (Serves 3)

Because she is such an active girl Judy doesn't always have time to sit down with the family for meals. She usually goes dashing out the door almost as soon as she's showered and changed after a day at the studio, so her mother tries to have on hand nutritious foods that Judy can nibble on. One of Mrs. Norton's favorite ways of getting Judy to eat right is to put a lot of healthy foods together in a salad.

Egg Salad Plus

3 hard-cooked eggs
Salt to taste
1 tablespoon minced green pepper
¼ cup diced celery
½ cup cottage cheese
1 tablespoon sour cream

Chop eggs or put through the large side of a grater. Add salt, green pepper and celery. Mix cottage cheese with sour cream until thoroughly blended. Toss with eggs and chill. Serve on crackers or party rye. This is a great way to provide a balanced meal that can be served quickly and easily. (Serves 6-8)

Another favorite salad, especially with those who have a sweet tooth, is this one. It goes well with chicken or turkey because it's light and delicate.

Ambrosia

2 large oranges, peeled and sectioned	2 tablespoons confectioners' sugar
2 firm bananas, cut into slices	¼ cup flaked coconut
1 8-ounce can pineapple chunks, drained and juice reserved	½ cup whipped cream or whipped topping
	¼ cup toasted almonds

Using a large bowl, alternately layer orange slices, bananas, and pineapple chunks. Sprinkle each layer with sugar and coconut. Pour reserved pineapple juice over layered fruit and chill for about 30 minutes. Remove from refrigerator and toss well with whipped cream.

Spoon into individual sherbet glasses. Sprinkle with toasted almonds. Chill for about 3 hours before serving. (Serves 6)

Men don't usually go for salads unless they're filled with stick-to-the-ribs ingredients. Turkey goes a long way, especially at holiday time, but no matter how many you have over for dinner or how small the turkey is there's usually enough left over for a delicious salad. Ralph Waite loves turkey. A real treat for him is one you can prepare with ease, certain that the man in your household will never say no to salad again.

Turkey Macaroni Salad

1 8-ounce package shell macaroni, cooked and drained
4 stalks celery, sliced
1 small red onion, chopped
½ cup chopped green pepper
3 cups diced cooked turkey
1 red apple, cored and cut into bite-sized pieces
Seasoned salt to taste
Mayonnaise
Salad greens
Paprika
Black olives, pitted and halved (optional)

Combine the first six ingredients in a large bowl. Season to taste. Toss with just enough mayonnaise to moisten. Cover and refrigerate until chilled. Serve on a bed of salad greens. Sprinkle lightly with paprika and garnish with pitted black olives, halved, if desired. (Serves 6)

Salads with a Spanish flavor go over big with members of the Walton family. This one is especially good served with cold roast beef.

Salad Espanol'

½ cup cooked garbanzo beans
1 small jar marinated artichoke hearts, drained thoroughly
1 small can hearts of palm
1 cup steamed cauliflower
1 cup steamed green beans
Romaine lettuce
Garlic salt to taste
¼ cup olive oil (or to taste)

Arrange the vegetables in layers on a medium-sized serving platter lined with romaine lettuce. Sprinkle with garlic salt and drizzle just enough olive oil over vegetables to lightly coat them.

A simpler way to serve this is to toss all the ingredients, except the olive oil, in a bowl. Add oil just before serving and toss again. Raw mushrooms and any fresh steamed vegetable you prefer can be added to this salad. (Serves 4)

A snappy flavored coleslaw gets the vote from the men on "The Waltons." The secret ingredients give it a unique taste. DAVID HARPER *(Jim-Bob) likes the crunchiness best of all.*

Snappy Coleslaw Crunch

¾ cup mayonnaise or cooked salad dressing
3 tablespoons sugar
3 tablespoons lemon juice
2 tablespoons milk
8 cups shredded green cabbage

2 large carrots, grated
½ cup diced, unpeeled red apples
2 oranges, peeled and cut into bite-sized pieces
½ cup Spanish peanuts

Combine mayonnaise, sugar and lemon juice and blend on low speed of blender for just a minute or two. Add milk and blend until smooth. Combine cabbage with carrots and apples. Pour dressing over this mixture making sure it is well coated. Chill for 30 minutes. Add orange pieces and nuts and toss again. Heap in your prettiest salad bowl and serve to compliments and requests for MORE. (Serves 8)

Even the simplest of salads can take on added glamour we're told by the imaginative Michael Learned. The trick is to serve salads well chilled with the greens dry and crisp, and to prepare and chill special dressings in advance so the seasonings can mingle. Chill salad plates in the refrigerator before serving, if you can.

The dressing is what puts the finishing touch on any salad. Here are several that are guaranteed to bring applause.

Blue Cheese Special

½ cup crumbled blue cheese (at room temperature)
1 cup sour cream
½ teaspoon seasoned salt
1 tablespoon minced onion
1 teaspoon lemon juice
¼ teaspoon Worcestershire sauce

Mash cheese. Mix with sour cream, salt and onion. Add lemon juice and Worcestershire sauce. Blend thoroughly and chill well before tossing with mixed greens. (Makes about 1½ cups)

Caraway Seed Dressing

¼ cup wine vinegar with garlic
1 tablespoon oil
1 tablespoon lemon juice
¼ cup tomato juice
¼ teaspoon dry mustard
Salt to taste
1 tablespoon sugar
1 cup mayonnaise
1 teaspoon minced onion
½ cup caraway seeds

In a medium-sized bowl combine vinegar, oil, lemon juice, tomato juice, mustard, salt, sugar and minced onion. Beat at medium speed for about 3 minutes. Add mayonnaise and beat another few minutes. Add caraway seeds and blend well. (Makes enough dressing to serve 8-10)

Snappy French Dressing (for greens)

½ cup wine vinegar
½ cup salad oil
 1 teaspoon garlic salt
¼ cup tomato juice
½ teaspoon each marjoram and thyme
Dash Tabasco sauce (optional)

Blend well in tight-lidded jar and chill. Shake before serving. (Makes enough dressing to serve 6)

When she has time on weekends Michael Learned likes to experiment with different ways of improvising on standard recipes.

Deluxe Waldorf Salad

 2 cups unpeeled, diced red apples
½ cup diced celery
 2 bananas, cut in thick slices (brush with lemon juice to prevent darkening)
½ cup dark raisins
¼ cup chopped walnuts
½ cup mayonnaise

In a medium-sized chilled bowl combine all the

ingredients. Toss well and chill thoroughly. Serve with slices of cold turkey and cheese breadsticks (Serves 4-6)

Fish in any form is not only high in protein, but also easy on the digestive system. When the members of the Walton family are at the studio they perform best if they eat just enough to sustain energy. As Richard Thomas says, "When you eat a big lunch the blood goes to your stomach to help digest it. That's why people get sleepy in the afternoon. An actor has to be alert. He needs to be wide awake to do his job well."

That goes for anyone who is out in the working world. So a favorite salad with a number of the cast members is:

Chef's Salmon Salad

Salad greens (escarole, watercress, romaine)
1 3½-ounce can pink salmon in chunks
2 slices of Swiss cheese, cut into julienne strips
8 cherry tomatoes
4 hard-cooked eggs, quartered
4 slices canned beets, cut into strips
Salt and coarse ground pepper to taste
French dressing
Lemon wedges

Tear greens into bite-sized pieces. Toss with other ingredients except dressing and lemon wedges in a chilled bowl. Just before serving add enough dressing to moisten. Garnish with lemon wedges and serve on a crisp bed of lettuce. (Serves 4)

Since Ellen Corby likes French food almost as well as Danish here's a salad dressing that is a combination of both tastes.

Danish French Combo Dressing

¼ cup wine vinegar (red with garlic is zestiest)
¼ cup lemon juice
¼ cup salad oil
2 tablespoons olive oil
Salt to taste
Dash each white pepper and cayenne pepper

1 clove garlic, minced
1 teaspoon sugar
½ cup mayonnaise
½ cup sour cream
¾ cup Danish blue cheese

Put all ingredients except cheese in an electric blender at medium speed for few seconds. Add crumbled cheese and whir again until well blended. (Yields 1½ cups)

6
Sandwiches

Weekends and late at night are when members of the Walton family put their imaginations to work dreaming up some wild concoctions in sandwiches. Of course, not everyone goes as far afield as Eric Scott, but sandwich making is a pastime the Waltons enjoy almost as much as sandwich eating.

Eric's Far OutWich

Spread crunchy peanut butter on 2 slices of egg bread. Arrange thin slices of dill pickle on 1 slice and cover with the second slice. Cut in half and, if you share Eric's tastes, munch your way through a delicious snack. Have plenty of your favorite icy cold juice on hand.

For another Eric Scott peanut butter fantasy spread smooth peanut butter on 1 slice of white bread. Cover with a layer of Rice Krispies. Cover with a plain slice of white bread and go to it.

Submarine Special

1 French roll, sliced in
  half lengthwise
Mild prepared mustard
1 slice Swiss cheese
1 slice American cheese

3 slices salami
2 slices bologna
Sliced cold chicken,
  turkey, lettuce or olives
  (as desired)

Sliced dill pickle
2 slices hard-cooked egg
 1 slice Bermuda onion
 1 slice beefsteak tomato
Salt to taste

Spread both sides of the roll with mustard. On one slice put cheese and meats in alternating layers, ending with the meat. Cover with dill pickle, egg, onion and tomato. Season to taste with salt. Place top half of roll over filling. Open wide and bite down carefully! If you wear braces skip this one.

Ralph Waite says there's nothing better than two slices of rye bread piled high with provolone cheese and hard salami. Spread hot mustard on one slice. For extra crunch and flavor add green pepper rings or thin slices of cucumber.

Sandwiches are really in with Jon Walmsley. He likes them hot and cold. Here are some of his favorites.

Hot Beef Steak San

1 hamburger bun, sliced and toasted
1 helping of leftover beef steak and onion (See recipe
  on page 78), piping hot
Hot gravy

Pile beef steak and onion mixture on bottom slice
of bun. Ladle gravy over all and top with other half
of bun.

Health Grill

2 slices enriched bread, buttered	1 slice tomato
2 slices sharp Cheddar cheese	Sliced avocado
1 lettuce leaf	Alfalfa sprouts
	Salt

Top each slice of bread with a slice of cheese.
Broil until cheese is melted. Remove to plate and
layer other ingredients on one slice. Season to taste.
Cover with second slice of bread. Anchor with toothpicks and cut in half.

Leftover Treat

2 slices dark rye bread
Barbecue sauce to cover 1 slice
Leftover cold turkey and roast beef

Put it all together and serve with a zesty coleslaw.

If you've never had a pork chop sandwich Jon says, you haven't tasted a really great sandwich filling.

Pork Chop Sandwich

Bibb lettuce
Soft roll, sliced
1 cold pork chop with bone removed per sandwich
Horseradish

Place lettuce leaf on bottom half of roll. Top with pork chop. Spread chop lightly with horseradish. Cover with top of roll. Serve with icy cold applesauce and gherkins.

No luncheon meat is ever served in the Mc-Donough home. Instead Mary's mom has plenty of leftover roast beef, turkey and baked ham on hand for sandwiches.

Mary's Favorites

Natural peanut butter spread thickly on honey berry bread. For extra goodness add very thin slices of unpared red apple and a sprinkle of cinnamon.

Ham *and* Sandwich

This one tastes best on whole-wheat bread. Lightly butter one slice. Cover a second slice of bread with mayonnaise or salad dressing. Cover buttered bread with a thick slice of baked ham, spread with cranberry sauce (Mary prefers her mother's homemade cranberry relish) and top with second slice of bread. Cut in half and add a few carrot sticks to munch on along with a cold glass of milk.

Ham sandwiches also taste great with thin slices of cucumber, sweet pickles and mustard spread in place of butter and mayonnaise.

Hearty roast beef sandwiches can't be beat. They get a big round of applause from the men on "The Waltons."

Basic Roast Beef San

2 slices caraway rye bread (per serving)
2 thin slices rare roast beef
1 lettuce leaf
Mustard
Thin sliced onion rings

For variations on this popular theme we received the following suggestions:

Slice a rye roll and spread with pickle relish. Top with roast beef and add slices of pitted ripe olives. Cover and enjoy!

Roast beef tastes really special on pumpernickel bread. Top one slice with lettuce, then add roast beef. Spread a small amount of chili sauce on meat. Cover with second slice of pumpernickel and garnish with dill pickles.

Horseradish spread over roast beef served with crunchy celery sticks is another winner.

If you were raised on Danish specialties like Ellen Corby then your taste will run to open-faced sandwiches with a light filling, served up attractively.

Salmon Triangles

1 3½-ounce can salmon, drained and flaked	Few drops lemon juice
	Mayonnaise to moisten
1 hard-cooked egg, finely chopped	1 radish, thinly sliced
	3 slices enriched white bread, with crusts removed, cut into triangles (3-4 per slice)
¼ teaspoon finely chopped ripe olives	
½ teaspoon diced celery	
Salt to taste	
Dash Worcestershire sauce	Parsley

Mix all the ingredients thoroughly except bread, radishes, parsley and small amount of ripe olives. Chill for 2-3 hours. Spread salmon mixture onto bread triangles. Top each with slice of radish and bits of chopped ripe olive. Garnish with sprigs of fresh parsley. (Serves 2).

If desired bread may be toasted before slicing. Toasted triangles should be spread lightly with butter before adding the salmon spread.

If you want to make David Harper (Jim-Bob) happy just serve up a hamburger or hot dog sandwich. He can eat them every day and never get tired of the taste. Of course, there are lots of ways to vary hamburger and hot dog sandwiches so that's no problem for his mom. If you or your children share this All-American taste, then try these variations for your own eating pleasure.

Basic Hamburgers

1 pound ground chuck or round steak
½ package onion soup mix
½ teaspoon garlic salt
¼ teaspoon seasoned pepper
¼ cup tomato sauce thinned with 1 tablespoon water

Mix all the ingredients thoroughly in a medium-sized bowl. Shape into 4 patties and pan fry or broil until done. (Serves 4)

Chili Con Carne Burgers

Toast 4 hamburger buns. Put a hamburger (see above) on bottom half of each bun. Top with home-made chili sauce (see recipe on page 79) and chopped onions. Cover with other half of bun. (Serves 4)

Cheese Melt Burger

Lightly butter bottom half of bun. Add hamburger patty and put under broiler. Top with 1 slice of Jack cheese and broil until melted. Add thin slices of green pepper and cover with top half of bun.

Saucy Burgers

2 tablespoons butter or oil
2 green onions, chopped
2 tablespoons chili sauce
1 teaspoon mustard

Melt butter and sauté onions. Remove and drain on paper towels. In small bowl mix chili sauce and mustard. Then add onions. Spoon over hamburgers (see recipe for Basic Hamburgers on page 65) and serve on 4 toasted buns.

Burgers and Fruit

Lightly sauté canned pineapple rings and sliced bananas in sweet butter. Sprinkle with nutmeg. Drain thoroughly. Add to hamburgers (see recipe for Basic Hamburgers on page 65). Serve on lightly buttered, toasted buns.

Variation: Using the same combination of pineapple and banana, omit butter and simmer the fruit in 2 tablespoons of soy sauce for a few minutes. Drain and serve as above.

Hot Dogs and Beans On A Bun

4 frankfurters
4 hot dog buns, split down the center and opened flat
1 8-ounce can vegetarian beans

1 tablespoon catsup
½ teaspoon mild prepared mustard
¾ cup brown sugar
¼ cup lemon juice

Make about four slashes in each frankfurter and grill.

Lightly grill buns.

While franks and buns are being grilled prepare the beans by mixing the remaining ingredients together and heating thoroughly in small saucepan. If too tangy add more brown sugar. Spread each bun with extra mustard, add hot dog and a tablespoon or two of bean mixture. (Serves 2-4)

Hot Diggity Hot Dog Sandwich

Split cooked frankfurter down middle. Spread 2 slices of pumpernickel with tangy mustard. Lay hot dog across 1 slice, add enough coleslaw to cover and top with second slice of bread.

Snappy Frank Sandwich

Slice crunchy French roll down the center. Spread small amount of chili sauce on bottom half. Add steamed frankfurter. Top with hot sauerkraut and sprinkle with caraway seeds.

Just Plain or Fancy Frank

Spread one half of split hot dog bun with pickle relish and the other with mustard. Add cooked frankfurter and any of the following trimmings (or eat as is):

Tomato slices
Cucumber slices
Sliced Cheddar cheese
Red onion rings
Hot peppers
Crisp bacon bits

7

Main Courses

"A happy family is but an earlier heaven." Bowring

Supper on "The Waltons" is always depicted as a time of family unity despite the little squabbles that occur among the seven Walton children. As Earl Hamner, Jr., the creator of the show says, "There is a bit of friction in every big family. Like all children we squabbled and bickered occasionally." But the underlying love and devotion they felt for one another gave them the sense of security they needed to overcome the hardships of the depression. On the television screen the Walton children may not display affection for one another by hugging and kissing. Instead the younger Waltons show their love and concern for one another in more subtle ways. Sisters often run off to play hand in hand; a brother may casually drape his arm across another brother's shoulder in a gesture of comraderie. Elizabeth is always included in whatever the older children are doing and she is looked after with loving consideration as the baby of the family.

The Walton kids may have their disagreements,

but none of the millions of viewers of the show can doubt that they really love one another.

"There never seemed to be any lack of conversation," Hamner remembers. "Everybody talked at once. We ate at a long wooden table with benches on each side, just as the Waltons do. Everybody was interested in what everybody else had to say about the happenings of the day."

Michael Learned and Ralph Waite who play the parents of the seven Walton children both had a great deal of practice in mothering and fathering within their own family units when they were growing up.

"My father was sent to the Aleutian Islands off Alaska for a year or so during World War II," Ralph Waite remembers. "I was in junior high, but because I was the eldest I was sort of head of the family during that time. It was my job to see that my sisters and brothers helped our mother with the dishes, set the table, etc. It was a tough time in many ways with the war and rationing." But memories of family closeness, of those lively dinnertime discussions and of his mother's good cooking far overshadow any hardships they may have had.

As the eldest of six daughters, Michael Learned was big sister and surrogate mother to the five younger ones. Today, with three sons of her own who are well on the way into manhood, family mealtime is still an important occasion. It is the time when she can relax with her sons as they relate the happenings of the day. They, in turn, are very interested in their mother's career and very proud of her.

"Because my house is small I don't entertain a lot of people at one time usually," Richard Thomas says. "I don't like to eat out and I don't like to eat

alone. I like to have dinner at my house with one or two close friends. When I was little our family always ate dinner together.

"That's probably why I don't like to eat alone. From the time I grew up dinner was always the time when the family got together and sat around the table talking over what happened that day. To me dinner is a social hour for talking over the day with friends or family."

Most of the members of the Walton family prefer simple but substantial meals after a day at the studio.

Ralph Waite's Old-Fashioned Pot Roast Favorite with Potatoes

1 clove garlic, peeled
3- to 4-pound boneless chuck or rump roast of beef
Flour
Salad oil
2 tablespoons seasoned salt
¾ cup water
1 bay leaf (optional)
6-8 new potatoes, peeled halved
Paprika

Rub garlic over meat. Coat well with flour and brown slowly in a heavy pan or Dutch oven using small amount of salad oil. Sprinkle with seasoned salt, turn and do the same on other side. Lower flame to simmer and add water and a bay leaf. Cover with a close fitting lid. Cook for 2-2½ hours. During final 45 minutes of cooking add potatoes that have been lightly salted. Sprinkle roast and potatoes with paprika and add more water if necessary at this time. (Serves 6-8)

Serve piping hot with Perfect Gravy (see page 72) to ladle over meat and potatoes.

PERFECT GRAVY

  2-4 tablespoons flour

  ½ cup cold water

1½ cups liquid from roast (after skimming off fat)
    add water if necessary

  1 tablespoon onion soup mix

In a small pan blend 1-2 tablespoons flour with cold water, stirring carefully to dissolve any lumps. Stir in pan juices, add the remaining flour and continue stirring until the flour and liquid are completely blended. Add onion soup mix and cook over a low flame until gravy thickens.

On the set where the "mothers" of the kids on the show spend time together knitting, crocheting, doing needlepoint and crewel work to pass the long day, there's a great feeling of companionship. State law requires that all child actors under the age of 18 must be accompanied by a parent or an adult acting as a parent while at the studio. Jon Walmsley's mom lost her "job" as chaperone when he reached his 18th birthday in February, 1974. But the other five Walton youngsters are still under parental supervision while working.

Turning out afghans, sweaters, and embroidered shirts keeps their hands busy. Socializing takes up a lot of time and helps keep the day from dragging for mothers of Eric Scott, Judy Norton and Mary Elizabeth McDonough. Kami Cotler, who plays Elizabeth, and David Harper, who is Jim-Bob, have set sitters to make sure the rules and regulations set down by the actors' union for child actors are enforced. It's not surprising that a lot of conversation is centered around food and diet. Everyone is more conscious about what they're eating these days. Exchanging recipes is a fun part of the routine for the mothers. Chicken and fish are especially popular with the cast of "The Waltons."

Polynesian Chicken Wings

2 pounds chicken wings, tips removed
Salt
1 cup sliced celery
1 green pepper, cut into strips
3-4 tablespoons butter or 2 tablespoons oil
1 chicken bouillon cube, dissolved in 1 cup water
½ cup soy sauce
Flour (enough to make paste or thicken)
2 8-ounce cans crushed pineapple
Shredded coconut
Mandarin orange or pineapple slices
Pinch ginger (optional)

Season chicken wings to taste with salt. Set in a buttered rectangular baking dish. In a skillet sauté celery and green pepper in hot butter or oil until crisp. Make a paste of bouillon (allow to cool first), soy sauce and flour.

Stir in pineapple and add additional flour if necessary to thicken slightly. Cover chicken with celery and green pepper. Pour pineapple sauce over all.

Bake in a preheated 300° oven, basting chicken wings with sauce and turning pieces every 10 minutes until chicken is tender, about 1 hour.

Serve sprinkled with shredded coconut and garnished with slices of mandarin orange or pineapple. For an extra snap to this tropical dish add a pinch

of ginger to the sauce before pouring over chicken.
(Serves 6-8)

Honeyed Chicken

Orange or sage honey
  2 cups raw wheat germ
  2 tablespoons chopped fresh parsley
  ¼ teaspoon thyme
  ¼ teaspoon basil
  1 3-pound chicken, cut up

Pour honey into a medium-sized bowl. On a separate platter or double thickness of paper towel mix
the remaining ingredients except the chicken until
well blended. Preheat oven to 350°.

Roll pieces of chicken in honey. Dip into wheat
germ mixture and bake for about 1 hour. (Serves 4-
6)

Japanese-Style Spareribs

2 pounds spareribs	1 teaspoon dry mustard
½ cup vinegar	Dash M.S.G.
2 tablespoons Worcester-shire sauce	Garlic salt and pepper to taste
2 tablespoons sugar	2 tablespoons brown sugar
½ cup catsup	

In a medium-sized glass or pyrex dish bake spareribs at 325°. Mix remaining ingredients except
brown sugar in a bowl and set aside. While spareribs are baking keep draining off fat and turning
them about every 15 minutes.

When ribs have baked for 40 minutes, remove

from oven and pour sauce over them. Sprinkle with
brown sugar. Cook an additional hour and 20 minutes adding small amounts of brown sugar and basting occasionally. (Serves 2-3)

This sauce is also delicious over chicken.

Chicken Stroganoff

1 3-pound chicken, cooked	¼ pound fresh mushrooms, sliced
½ cup plus 3 tablespoons flour	¼ cup lemon juice
Salt to taste	½ cup chicken broth or 1 cup chicken bouillon cube dissolved in ½ cup water
½ tablespoon paprika	
¼ cup butter	¾ cup sour cream

Cut meat from chicken in chunks. Set aside 3
tablespoons flour. Put ½ cup flour in plastic bag
along with seasonings. Add chicken and shake to
coat well. Brown chicken pieces in melted butter.
Remove from heat. Dip sliced mushrooms in lemon
juice and sauté in butter in a separate skillet. Remove from heat.

In small bowl mix flour with broth gradually,
stirring well to avoid lumps. Pour over chicken in
skillet and return to stove. Cook over medium heat,
stirring continuously until thickened. Stir in sour
cream, then mushrooms. Simmer for an additional
5-10 minutes and serve immediately over hot rice.
(Serves 4)

Orange-Teriyaki Chicken

2 2½-pound fryer chickens, cut up in eighths
Salt to taste
¼ cup orange juice
¼ cup teriyaki sauce
1 teaspoon grated orange peel

Arrange chickens in a lightly greased shallow pan
or baking sheet (use sweet butter). Season lightly
with salt to your family's taste. Mix orange juice
and teriyaki sauce in small bowl and brush on each
piece of chicken with pastry brush, making certain
to coat chicken thoroughly with the sauce. Bake,
skin side up in a preheated 375° oven for 30
minutes. Turn chicken and brush on remainder of
sauce. Bake an additional 20 minutes. Sprinkle
with grated orange rind and bake 10 more minutes
or until chicken is tender and crisp. (Serves 8)

*Sunday dinner is a special occasion at the
Walmsley's. Jon's father is a sales manager, and his
job requires him to deal with people all week long.
Weekends are for quiet relaxing. Traditional English dinners are served on Sundays. Table talk is
generally catching up on what each member of the
family is doing. A lot of discussion is about television.*

*"We always watch the first airing of each Walton
show," Jon told us. Although he gets no criticism
from his parents, Jon admitted "I pull myself to
pieces all of the time."*

*English cooking is plain, but hearty. They don't
use a lot of spices in their cooking. However, a din-*

*ner of roast beef, Yorkshire pudding, baked potatoes
and mixed vegetables can't be beat in Jon's opinion.
Unless it's a mixed grill or roast lamb dinner.*

Plain Yorkshire Pudding

1 cup all-purpose flour
Pinch salt
2 eggs
1 cup milk

Spoon off drippings from roast to measure ½ cup
and pour into heated 9x9x2 inch pan.

Put floor in small bowl and add salt. Break in eggs
and mix well to dissolve all lumps. Gradually add
milk until desired thickness for pudding is reached.
Let stand for about 15 minutes before pouring into
baking pan. Bake in hot oven, 400°-450°, for 30-
45 minutes.

For extra flavor Yorkshire pudding can be baked
right in pan along with roast during last half hour
or so.

Mixed Grill

2 pounds boneless steak	4-8 link sausages
4 pork chops	Salt to taste
1 pound calves' liver, sliced thinly	8-12 mushrooms, whole with stems
4-8 slices bacon	2 tomatoes

Grease the broiler lightly and preheat. Broil pork
chops first as they take the longest. Add steak, sau-
sage, liver and bacon. Season meat to taste. Add

mushrooms and tomato at the very last for about 5
minutes. Serve on a heated platter. (Serves 4)

Beefsteak Pan Pie

  1 tablespoon flour
  ¼ teaspoon salt
  ¼ teaspoon pepper
1½ pounds boneless round steak or lean chuck
  1 medium onion, chopped
  ½ cup Burgundy wine (optional)

Mix flour with salt and pepper. Cut steak into
bite-sized pieces and roll in flour mixture until well
coated. Put in a heavy stewpan. Add onion and
enough water to cover. Cook over a medium flame
for 1½ hours. Add more water if needed during
cooking time. For added zip stir in ½ cup robust
red wine.

If desired thicken gravy with small amount of
flour. Make a crust of your favorite dumpling mixture. Place crust on top of steak and cook, uncovered for 10 minutes. Cover pan and cook
additional 10 minutes. (Serves 3-4)

This is almost the same recipe as the one for
steak and kidney pie (see page 34) except for the
variation in crust and omitting the kidneys. However
the taste of the steak and onions with the dumpling
crust is delightful. You may want to vary your
dumpling crust by adding crushed herbs, parsley
flakes or even grated cheese to the dough for a
special flavor.

What KAMI COTLER *(Elizabeth) likes best of all are the good things her father barbecues for dinner. Outdoor barbecuing is a southern California pastime enjoyed by many of the Waltons.*

Barbecued Spareribs

4 pounds spareribs, parboiled and lightly salted
3 cups Barbecue Sauce

Barbecue Sauce

½ cup salad oil
1 tablespoon prepared mustard
1 8-ounce can tomato sauce
2 tablespoons finely chopped white onion
2 tablespoons Worcester-shire sauce

1 tablespoon flour
Dash pepper
½ cup catsup
½ cup lemon juice or white vinegar
½-1 teaspoon liquid hickory smoke
3-4 tablespoons brown sugar

Put ingredients in a blender or tightly covered quart jar. Add sugar last, gradually, taste testing since the amount of sweetness desired varies with each individual.

Heat ingredients that have been shaken in jar or blended thoroughly in blender and simmer until heated through. Put spareribs on coals and brush sauce on top. Turn every 20 minutes, basting with sauce, until done. (Serves 4-6)

Although she's just learning to cook, Kami is looking forward to the day when she can prepare something simple all by herself. Recently Kami made her cooking debut by making a batch of pancakes (with her mom's help) for Sunday breakfast. Kami says they came out "okay." She is proud of the fact that she can "crack a mean egg." For those of us who haven't yet mastered the trick of cracking an egg without breaking the yolk or getting bits of shell into the bowl, that's an achievement to applaud in a nine-year-old novice cook.

Second best to her father's barbecue specialties Kami loves chop suey.

Chicken Chop Suey

2 whole chicken breasts, boned with skin removed	½ cup sliced scallions
1 teaspoon salt	1½ cups chicken broth
3½ tablespoons salad oil	1 tablespoon soy sauce
1 cup diagonally sliced celery	1 tablespoon corn starch
½ cup sliced fresh mushrooms	¼ cup cold water
1 small can water chestnuts	1 1-pound can bean sprouts, drained well
	½ cup toasted slivered almonds
	4 cups hot rice

Cut chicken into bite-sized chunks. Add salt to oil and heat in a skillet. Stir in chicken and sauté until lightly browned. Add celery, mushrooms, scallions, water chestnuts and chicken broth. Cook over medium heat, covered tightly, for about 10 minutes.

Make a paste by blending soy sauce, cornstarch

and cold water in a cup. Remove lid from chicken and slowly add soy sauce mixture, stirring gently. Add bean sprouts and cook an additional few minutes then sprinkle with almonds. Serve very hot over chinese noodles. Additional bottled soy sauce may be passed for extra flavor. (Serves 4-6)

High in nutrition, yet light but filling is this family favorite of Michael's.

Aunt Bev's Stuffed Fish Supreme

½ white onion, chopped	1 egg, beaten
1 tablespoon cooking oil	1-2 pounds fillet of sole
1 3½-ounce can red salmon, well drained with bones removed	(large enough to roll up)
½ cup fine cracker crumbs	Flour

Sauté onions in small amount of oil until golden. In a small bowl mix salmon with cracker crumbs and egg. Add onions and mix well.

Wash sole, dry thoroughly with paper towels and lightly dust with flour. Spread salmon mixture over one side of fillet and roll up like a jelly roll. Anchor with toothpicks and place in rectangular baking dish. Make up sauce and pour over fish. (Serves 2-4)

SPECIAL SAUCE

¼ cup diced onions
½ green pepper, diced
2 tablespoons sweet butter
1 8-ounce can tomato sauce mixed with 1 can cold water
Dash salt and pepper

Sauté onions and green pepper in butter until soft. Stir in tomato sauce/water. Add salt and pepper to tomato mixture and pour over rolled up sole. Bake for 30 minutes in a preheated 375° oven. Slice and serve 3-4.

You haven't tasted anything quite like chicken baked in the oven with a savory homemade Italian (spaghetti) sauce, a fact we learned from Ralph Waite.

Chicken Italia

2 2½-pound chickens, cut up (freeze giblets and livers for another use)
Seasoned salt to taste
½ cup salad oil

Heat oil in a roasting pan large enough to hold chicken pieces without crowding. Sprinkle chicken parts lightly with seasoned salt. Place in pan and brown each piece of chicken lightly on both sides.

In the meantime have the following sauce made up.

SARA'S SAUCE

1½	cups chopped onion	1	tablespoon salt
1	green pepper, chopped	1	tablespoon sugar
½	pound fresh mushrooms, sliced	½	teaspoon black pepper
⅓	cup olive oil	1	tablespoon crushed oregano
2	cloves garlic, minced	2	bay leaves, crushed
2	#2½ cans (or 7 cups) stewed tomatoes	1	teaspoon basil
2⅔	cups tomato paste	2	cups dry red Burgundy wine

Sauté onion, green pepper and mushrooms in hot oil until tender and golden in color. Add all seasonings gradually along with the remaining ingredients except the wine. Simmer, uncovered, for about 2 hours, stirring occasionally. Add wine and simmer an additional 2 hours so all flavors are well blended and sauce is thickened.

Pour sauce over chicken pieces and bake in a preheated slow oven, 300°, for about 1 hour. Cook an 8-ounce package of manicotti shells according to package directions and serve with chicken and extra sauce poured over all. (Serves 6-8 heartily.)

What tastes extra special on a rainy California night? The kids on the show agree that chili is the perfect dreary weather dinner.

Really Robust Chili Con Carne

1 cup chopped onion
1 large green pepper, chopped
3 tablespoons salad oil
1 clove garlic, minced
1½ pounds ground chuck beef
1-pound 12-ounce can tomatoes
½ teaspoon salt

2 tablespoons chili powder (more if you like it really hot)
1 teaspoon paprika
Dash cayenne pepper.
3 1-pound cans red chili beans or kidney beans
Tomato juice or water (optional)
Chopped onion for garnish (optional)

In a Dutch oven or large skillet gently cook onion and green pepper in 3 tablespoons oil until golden and tender. Add garlic and meat and brown, stirring with a fork to prevent clumping. Add tomatoes and salt (taste to see if additional salt is needed), chili powder, paprika and cayenne.

Simmer for 2 hours, uncovered. Add beans and heat thoroughly. If necessary add tomato juice or small amount of water at this time to give proper consistency. Season further with chili powder to taste and mix through before serving in individual bowls with chopped onion sprinkled on top of each serving (optional). Great with crusty French or Italian bread.

Here are more Walton favorites.

Crunchy Buttermilk Chicken

1 cup buttermilk
1 egg, slightly beaten
1 cup flour
1 cup finely chopped
pecans
½ cup finely chopped
unsalted cashews

1 tablespoon salt
1 tablespoon paprika
Dash pepper
2 3-pound broilers, cut
up

Blend buttermilk with egg. On wax paper or a platter mix together flour, chopped nuts and seasonings. Lightly salt the chicken parts and dip first in the buttermilk then in the flour mixture. Arrange chicken pieces, skin side down, in a large foil-lined baking pan. Bake in a preheated 350° oven for 30 minutes then turn chicken skin side up and bake 30-45 minutes longer, until chicken is tender. (Serves 6-8)

Shrimp Paella

1 pound cooked shrimp
1 16-ounce can tomatoes
1 tablespoon finely
minced onion
1 teaspoon paprika

1 chicken bouillon cube
1 cup uncooked instant
rice
Dash cayenne

Stir all ingredients together in large heavy frying pan. Heat to boiling, stirring now and then. Simmer for a few minutes. Remove from fire, cover and let stand about 10 minutes or until rice has absorbed sufficient liquid. (Serves 5)

Halibut Steaks In Wine Sauce

½ cup chopped onion

½ cup chopped green pepper

1 clove garlic, crushed

2 tablespoons sweet butter

¾ cup dry white wine

Salt and pepper to taste

1 teaspoon crushed basil leaves

1 8-ounce can stewed tomatoes

4 fresh halibut steaks

Seasoned salt

Sauté onion, green pepper and garlic in melted butter until tender. Add all other ingredients but halibut. Bring to slow boil and simmer for 15 minutes. Butter a baking dish large enough to hold halibut steaks. Sprinkle halibut with seasoned salt. Pour sauce over fish. Cover pan with foil and bake in a preheated oven for 15 minutes. Remove foil and baste fish. Bake, uncovered, for an additional 10 minutes, or until fish flakes. (Serves 4)

"I was sort of raised on Cuban food," Richard Thomas says. *"My mother and I both cook Cuban dishes well. It's mellower than Spanish food which uses more tomato sauce and spices, and the Cubans use a lot of olive oil in their cooking."*

Here are two of Richard's favorite Cuban dishes.

Chicken and Rice

Olive oil
1 2½-pound fryer, cut up
2 cans beer plus ½ cup water
½ cup long-grain rice, rinsed and drained thoroughly
½ onion, thinly sliced
1 clove garlic, minced
2 medium-sized soft tomatoes, cut up
Dash cumin
Pimento strips
Cooked asparagus spears
Pitted black olives

In heavy skillet heat enough oil to fry chicken until browned. Add beer mixed with water and simmer, covered, for 30 minutes. Add rice and simmer, covered, until rice is done, 30-45 minutes.

In a separate pan sauté onion, garlic and tomatoes in 1-2 tablespoons hot olive oil, stirring carefully so it does not burn. Sprinkle with cumin and cook until golden brown. Add to chicken and simmer an additional 10 minutes, or until flavor of sauce has cooked through to the rice. Serve the chicken on a bed of rice. Garnish with strips of pimento, asparagus spears and pitted black olives. (Serves 4)

Frijoles Negros (Black Beans) and Rice

½ cup dried black beans
3 tablespoons olive oil or Spanish oil
½ cup green pepper, cut in strips
½ onion, thinly sliced
¼ teaspoon oregano
Salt to taste
½ clove garlic, minced
½ cup long-grain white rice, rinsed and well drained
1 teaspoon sugar

Soak dried beans overnight in water to cover. The following day bring beans to a boil in the same water. Heat oil in a frying pan and sauté other ingredients except rice and sugar. Prepare rice as directed on package while beans are cooking, salt to taste. When vegetables are golden brown, remove from fire and cover.

Cook beans until tender, 1-1½ hours. Purée beans by removing small quantities from the pot and mashing on a separate plate then return to pot. Continue on low boil until beans are thoroughly cooked. Add vegetables and sugar. Mix through and cook 5 more minutes. (Serves 4)

Some people like to mix the beans with the rice and serve it that way. Others prefer bean mixture served with hot rice in separate mound so they can mix it themselves. Whichever way you'll agree with Richard that this is a truly delicious meal in itself. Or you may want to serve it with what Richard refers to as his own method of cooking a very tasty hamburger.

Hamburger Divine

Seasoned salt to taste
 1 pound ground round steak
¼ pound sweet butter

Season meat in a bowl. Shape into four thickish hamburger patties. Melt butter until it starts to turn brown. Fry hamburgers, turning frequently, in deep butter sauce until butter turns black. (Serves 4)

Richard says that the trick is to get the skillet really hot before adding the butter. Hamburgers cooked this way come out nice and crisp on the outside and juicy on the inside.

French cooking delights Michael Learned and Ellen Corby, and they both agree this chicken cooked in wine is extra good.

Coq Au Vin

3-6 slices bacon, diced
2 tablespoons sliced green onion
2 tablespoons butter
1 2½- to 3-pound broiler, cut up
8 whole boiling onions, peeled
1 cup sliced mushrooms
1 clove garlic, minced

Salt and pepper to taste
¼ teaspoon thyme
1 stalk celery, with leaves
1 bay leaf
2 cups Burgundy wine
1 cup chicken broth
2 sprigs fresh parsley, chopped

Brown bacon and green onion in a Dutch oven. Remove and drain thoroughly. Add butter to bacon drippings and brown chicken over low flame, turning frequently. Remove chicken and set aside. Pour off most of fat in pot. Add to pot white onions, mushrooms, garlic, bacon and onions. Return chicken to pot and season with salt and pepper to taste, turning once. Sprinkle with thyme. Add celery, bay leaf and wine. Simmer for 10 minutes, add broth. Add parsley, stir through and cover again before placing in a preheated 350° oven for 2 hours. (Serves 4)

A flavorful stew is a family favorite with Mary Elizabeth McDonough, and Jon Walmsley's mom prepares stew frequently during the winter months. Stew was served often during the boyhood of Earl Hamner, Jr. because it stretched such a long way. On the farm where he grew up Will Geer loved the taste of fresh vegetables his mother cooked in stew. Served with dumplings of fresh baked biscuits, it's a meal few people can resist, and for some reason stew always seems to taste even better the second day.

Stew à la Waltons

1 tablespoon cooking oil
½ cup sliced fresh mushrooms
1 large white onion, sliced
1 teaspoon seasoned salt
1 cup flour
2 pounds bottom round, cut in 1-inch cubes
2 yams, peeled and thickly sliced
2 cups tomato juice
1 cup water
½ cup Burgundy wine (optional)
1 bay leaf
¼ teaspoon dried marjoram
Dash freshly ground pepper
6 potatoes, peeled and cut in chunks
6 carrots, scraped and thickly sliced
1 cup fresh corn niblets
1 cup sliced fresh zucchini

Heat the oil sauté mushrooms, and onions until just tender. On paper towel or wax paper add seasoned salt to flour. Lightly season meat and coat well with flour mixture before adding to pan with mushrooms and onions. Brown meat well. Transfer to a 3-quart Dutch oven or heavy kettle. Add yams,

tomato juice, water, wine and bay leaf. Sprinkle
with marjoram and pepper. Simmer, uncovered, for
1 hour. Add additional juice or water, if necessary,
during simmering time. Add potatoes, carrots and
corn niblets. Cover and simmer an additional 30
minutes. Add zucchini and steam 5 minutes. Stir
through stew before serving on bed of hot noodles.
(Serves 6.)

*International flavor in foods is an adventure many
of the Waltons enjoy.*

Gourmet Eggplant Dinner

1 large eggplant	¼ pound mushrooms, thinly sliced
½ cup diced onions	Dash oregano
½ cup diced shallots	½ pound fresh crabmeat chunks
1 tablespoon olive oil	¼ cup grated Parmesan cheese
½ pound baby shrimp, cooked and shelled	¼ cup fine seasoned bread crumbs
2 firm tomatoes, cut in small pieces	
½ cup diced green pepper	

Cut eggplant in half and scoop out inside leaving
shell one-half inch thick. Cut up eggplant pulp and
cook in boiling salted water for 10 minutes. Drain
and set aside.

Sauté onions and shallots in olive oil, then add
shrimp, tomatoes, green pepper and mushrooms.
Cook in oil until soft. Sprinkle with fresh or dried
oregano and mix through. Add crabmeat and cooked
eggplant. Pile into eggplant shell.

Springle with grated parmesan cheese and bread crumbs. Bake at 350° for 45 minutes. (Serves 4)

At 13 David Harper (Jim-Bob) is already looking to the future. Affectionately nicknamed "Little Scrambler" by the crew of "The Waltons" (because he seems to be everywhere at the same time), David and some of his close friends are already at work on making a film of their own. That's what David wants to be when he grows up: a film maker. Born in Abilene, Texas, David comes from a show biz family. His dad, Paul Harper, is a well-known character actor. Bunny, his mom, is a song writer.

When David sits down to dinner at home he always hopes it will be one of his favorites: spaghetti with meat balls, pizza or tacos, with jello or chocolate pudding for dessert.

David's Italian Meat Balls 'N Spaghetti

MEATBALLS:

1 pound ground beef
½ cup seasoned bread crumbs
1 egg, well beaten
1 clove garlic, finely chopped
½ cup chopped onion
Salt and pepper to taste

3 tablespoons chopped fresh parsley
¼ cup Parmesan cheese, grated
Pinch nutmeg
½ teaspoon crushed oregano
6 tablespoon salad oil

Combine all ingredients except oil. Shape into 1 inch balls. Fry in hot oil until browned. Set aside. Reheat before serving or keep warm on low flame until ready to serve.

MEAT SAUCE FOR SPAGHETTI:

2 tablespoons salad oil	½ clove minced garlic
½ pound ground beef	½ teaspoon basil
½ cup canned tomatoes	Salt to taste
½ cup minced onion	

Heat oil. Add ground meat and cook gently until all redness is gone. Add other ingredients. Stir through and cook for about 20 minutes on simmer flame.

Cook up 8 ounces spaghetti. Drain and serve on large platter with spaghetti sauce and meatballs. (Serves 4-6)

A boyhood supper treat, and one that Will Geer often prepares for his own family tastes just as good to him today as it did years ago in Indiana. Will Geer's first love is acting, and the family tradition is being carried on by his two sons Tad and Raleigh, his daughters Ellen and Kate, and Ellen's son Ian. Acting has captivated the third generation. So has "Grandpa's" good cooking judging from this recipe.

Jambalaya

1 pound ground beef	1 cup cooked rice
1 onion, chopped	1 green pepper, sliced
1 tablespoon oil	½ cup okra (optional)
Salt to taste	¼ cup grated mozzarella
Dash rosemary	cheese

Brown meat and onions in hot oil. Season with salt and rosemary. In a buttered 2-quart casserole dish layer ingredients starting with rice, green pepper strips or rings, meat-onion mxture and okra. Top with grated mozzarella cheese and bake for 1 hour in a preheated 350° oven. (Serves 4)

Another healthy main dish that's very basic and nourishing is one Will Geer often cooks for his troupe of actors, who tour in an old Greyhound bus bringing Shakespeare, the outdoors and an enrapt audience together. This past summer Will and his troupe held an all-day Garden Theater Festival that ran for five days. People who attended the event, held in a wooded area tucked into a winding canyon neear Hollywood, walked on a carpet of herbs. Rosemary, savory, thyme and mint were planted with loving care by Will and grew in fragrant abundance making a lush carpet on which to tread.

Tuna Dinner

1 large yellow squash
Turnip greens
1 family-size can chunk-style tuna
Savory

Wash and cut squash in cubes. Steam in small amount of boiling salted water along with turnip greens. Cook, covered, until just tender (no more than 10 minutes). Drain off oil or water from tuna. Add and toss with steamed vegetables, sprinkle with savory and serve as is.

8

Vegetables
Everyone Will Love

―――――――

Getting kids and husbands to eat their vegetables is no easy task. From the members of the Walton family we've gathered together ways and means of turning your family on to the good taste in vegetables—yes, even spinach.

Will Geer said this about his feelings on food, especially vegetables:

"After a long day of filming, Ol' Grandpa likes a good well-balanced meal, although with my busy schedule I usually don't have the time or temperament of Chef Boy-ar-dee! My evenings are filled with personal appearances, reading new scripts or rehearsing my Shakespearean troupe for our weekend performances at my outdoor theater in Topanga Canyon. The theater doubles as somewhat of a garden paradise where I grow most of the vegetables I eat.

"When I march into the house evenings, the first thing I do (after dropping my faithful Indian carry-

95

all bag) is to start a pot of water boiling, with never a preconceived idea of what's for dinner . . . . . until I open the refrigerator door.

"Broccoli is a favorite of mine and with my special Cheddar cheese sauce even my finicky Walton grandchildren would find it hard to hide this under their napkins."

Grandpa Walton's Broccoli and Cheddar

1 pound fresh broccoli, trimmed	1 tablespoon yeast
2 cups milk	½ teaspoon herb salt
¼ cup flour	½ pound bulk sharp Cheddar cheese, cut in cubes
2 tablespoons butter or margarine	

Add broccoli to boiling salted water and cook until just tender, about 10 minutes. Drain and set aside.

Heat milk in small saucepan and stir in enough flour to make a thin paste. Mix through with butter, yeast and herb salt. Add cheese and stir until melted. Put broccoli into a buttered one-quart casserole dish and fold in cheese sauce. Bake for 25-30 minutes at 375°. (Serves 4)

Our herb expert cautions that most herbs need a lot of sun, all but mint. And take care not to overwater your herb garden.

Steamed parsley and steamed pigweed, a member of the amaranth family, are two of Grandpa's vegetable favorites. Add a dash of herbs while steaming vegetables and you'll probably work that miracle with your own family.

Eric Scott's mom gets him to eat green beans by doing just that—a dash of garlic powder or oregano while the beans are cooking makes all the difference, she says.

Mary Elizabeth's mother turns a vegetable like peas into a chef's delight.

Italian-Style Peas

½ onion, chopped
1 tablespoon cooking oil
½ cup diced fresh tomatoes
2 cups fresh peas, steamed with liquid retained
Grated Parmesan cheese

In a saucepan brown onions in one tablespoon oil. Add tomatoes and cook for about 3 minutes.

Mash a few peas in the pot to thicken liquid. Add peas, onions and tomatoes and simmer for 8-10 minutes. Serve in a bowl topped with grated Parmesan cheese. (Serves 6)

Judy Norton's family often makes a meal of vegetables. No seasoning is used so the true flavor of the vegetables comes through.

Vegetable Dinner

1 tablespoon butter or margarine	1 cup cut-up cauliflower
½ onion, diced	½ small head red cabbage, cut into wedges
½ cup sliced fresh mushrooms	½ cup sliced fresh zucchini
¼ cup diced celery	1 cup bean sprouts
2 carrots, pared and diced	Small bunch spinach, well washed and drained
½ cup sliced banana squash	Grated mild cheese

Melt butter in a large tight-lidded pan or electric fry pan with lid. Sauté onion, mushrooms, celery and carrots until golden in uncovered pan. Add banana squash, cauliflower and red cabbage and steam, covered, for about 15 minutes, or until vegetables begin to turn slightly soft. Add zucchini and bean sprouts and steam an additional 5 minutes. Add spinach and steam about 2 minutes. Mix through so all vegetables are thoroughly blended together. While still hot sprinkle with grated cheese of your choice and let cheese melt before serving. (Serves 4)

"When I get home at night I just heat some vegetables, usually zucchini," Ellen Corby told us.

Zucchini Provençal

1 zucchini
Few slices onion
½ clove garlic
Pinch each oregano and basil
½ fresh tomato, chopped

Thinly slice well scrubbed zucchini. Cook with onions in water to cover to which garlic clove and herbs have been added. When tender, but still crisp, add tomato. Heat until tomato is soft and flavors are blended well. Drain and remove garlic before serving. (Serves 1)

Ellen is also a parsley fan and tries to eat some raw or cooked every day along with zucchini or any other fresh cooked vegetable.

Kami's favorite vegetable is artichokes. She loves them steamed in boiling salted water until tender then dipped in butter. But for a special gourmet touch our Walton cooking specialists provided this recipe.

Terri's Artichoke Treat

4 artichokes

Equal amounts seasoned bread crumbs, grated Parmesan and Romano cheeses (amount depends upon size of artichokes)

3 garlic cloves, peeled and finely chopped

Dash coarse ground pepper

4 tablespoons olive oil

Trim artichokes and cut off stems. Carefully spread leaves apart for stuffing, (If artichokes resist spreading leaves apart, hit against side of the sink and they will comply at once.) Mix ingredients, except for oil, in bowl and stuff inside of each artichoke leaf with a tablespoon or so of mixture. Set in a small amount water and steam for about 20 minutes. Remove artichokes from water. Place in another pot and pour olive oil over them until well saturated. Steam until tender, about 40 minutes depending upon size of artichokes. (Serves 4)

Spinach is rich in iron and other good minerals, but try to get hubby and kids to eat it. That's another story we all know by heart. Kids and grown-ups on "The Waltons" like their spinach dressed up. Maybe your family will, too.

Spinach Surprise

    1 cup plain yogurt
    ½ envelope dried onion soup mix
    2½ pounds cooked fresh spinach, well drained
    2 teaspoon grated mild Cheddar cheese

Add yogurt and soup mix to cooked spinach and mix together thoroughly, but with a delicate touch. Put in a lightly buttered 1-quart casserole and sprinkled with cheese. Bake for 30 minutes in a preheated 350° oven. (Serves 6.)

Hong Kong Spinach

¼ -½ cup butter
Salt and pepper to taste
    1 small can water chestnuts
    2 tablespoons minced onion
    ¼ cup lemon juice
    2 tablespoons soy sauce
    2 pounds fresh spinach, washed and trimmed

Melt butter. Add seasonings, water chestnuts and onion. Cook over medium heat for about 2 minutes. Add lemon juice that has been blended with soy sauce. Put spinach in a medium-sized saucepan with above mixture and steam until tender. About 5 minutes of steaming is usually sufficient. Don't overcook as spinach should not be served limp. (Serves 4)

Spinach Patties

2 cups cooked spinach, chopped
1 egg, beaten
½ cup chopped onion
Enough bread or cracker crumbs to bind well
Salt to taste
Deep fat for frying

Mix spinach with egg and blend thoroughly. Add onion and enough bread crumbs so mixture will hold its shape during cooking. Season to taste. Heat fat in skillet and drop in 2 tablespoons of spinach mixture at a time to form patties. Brown on each side. Drain on paper towels. Serve to rave notices. (Makes 6-8 patties)

In France they say "oui oui" to crêpes. Our two French cooking enthusiasts, Ellen Corby and Michael Learned, think we might learn a lesson from the fine chefs of France. Here's a great way to transform an untempting green vegetable like spinach into a delectable dish merely by enfolding it carefully in a light, tasty crêpe.

Spinach Crepes

CREPES

2 eggs, well beaten with pinch salt
½ cup all-purpose flour, unsifted
1 tablespoon wheat germ (optional)
1 cup milk

Put all ingredients in blender and blend at medium speed until smooth. Chill in the refrigerator for 1 hour. Coat a crepe pan, 8-inch skillet or griddle with butter and heat until very hot. Pour enough crepe batter into pan (if using a griddle make 5-inch rounds) to cover bottom of pan with thin layer. Cook over high flame, shaking pan lightly to keep crepe from sticking. Cook until edges begin to turn brown and start to move away from pan. Turn crepe carefully and cook on other side until lightly browned. Remove crepe gently to clean towel. Allow to drain until all crepes are made. (Makes about 6 crepes)

FILLING

1½ pounds spinach, steamed until tender and chopped or	Dash cayenne pepper (optional)
1 pound broccoli, steamed and chopped finely	Salt to taste
	2 ounces shredded Cheddar cheese
½ onion, chopped	1 tablespoon butter
Dash marjoram	Chopped chives for garnish

Drain vegetable well. Heat small amount of butter in skillet and cook vegetable with onion until onion is tender. Add seasonings and cheese. Mix through and remove from heat.

In center of each crepe place 1 tablespoon of vegetable mixture. Roll up. Lightly butter a square baking dish large enough to hold all 6 crepes. Bake for 15 minutes at 425°.

Sprinkle with chopped chives before serving.

*Another mouth-watering way to entice your family
to eat their vegetables is to French fry them. Crunchy
treats can be made of eggplant, green pepper rings,
yams, and even parsnips. Zucchini breaded and fried
is a taste you'll never forget. Zucchini and eggplant
should be cut into finger-sized pieces and yams in
thin slices before frying.*

French Fry Batter For Vegetables

Ice water
Salad oil
1-2 eggs, well beaten with a small amount of water
 1 cup seasoned bread crumbs or 1 cup plain flour or
   pancake mix with herb seasoning to taste

Soak slices of vegetable in ice water to cover for
about 30 minutes. Remove from water and blot well
with paper towels. Heat oil in skillet. Dip each slice
of vegetable first in egg and then in crumbs or flour.
Fry in hot oil until crisp and browned on outside.
Drain well before serving. These may be kept hot
and crisp in a baking dish in a very slow oven until
ready to serve.

Carrot Goodies

4 carrots, pared and cut into large pieces
2 tablespoons apricot, peach or orange marmalade

Cook carrots until tender, but not too soft in boiling salted water. Arrange in a small buttered casserole. Melt marmalade in top of double boiler. Pour

over carrots and bake for 15–20 minutes at 350°.
(Serves 6)

Herbed Green Beans

½ onion, chopped	Dash marjoram
1 tablespoon cooking oil	1 teaspoon savory
½ pound green beans, cooked until tender	½ tomato, peeled and diced
Garlic salt to taste	

Sauté onion in oil until golden and soft. Add green beans, garlic salt and herbs. Steam, covered, for about 10 minutes. Add tomato and steam for an additional 3 minutes until tomato are soft. Mix through before serving. (Serves 4)

To add zip to such vegetables as broccoli, cauliflower and even spinach top with the following sauce.

Creamed Mustard

Add 1-2 teaspoons prepared mustard to your favorite cream sauce and stir well. Pour over steamed vegetables and bake at 300° until well blended and piping hot, about 10-15 minutes.

9

Holiday Dinners
and
Holiday Specialties

Although Christmas with turkey and all the trimmings won the majority of votes from members of the Walton family in the matter of favorite holiday dinners, there were a few differences in the choice of "all the trimmings" as well as votes for other holidays.

Christmas Goose with a very special giblet stuffing his mother taught him to make is what Richard Thomas cooks up for the three or four guests he invites to Christmas dinner. This is the time of year when Richard goes all out, not only cooking but also baking his own mince pie. As he says, "It only happens once a year."

Christmas Dinner At Richard's

Roast Goose
Giblet Dressing*
Sweet Potatoes with Marshallows*
Corn on the Cob
Mince Pie

* recipes given

Giblet Dressing

2 pounds bacon, fried very crisp and chopped into tiny pieces, grease reserved	Goose giblets
	2 cups sliced fresh mushrooms
	1 cup sliced fresh cucumber
6-7 loaves white bread, cut into very small pieces	1½ cups chopped onions
	1 tablespoon cooking oil
Poultry seasoning to taste (allow about 1 teaspoon per 12 cups of bread crumbs)	Salt and pepper

The night before mix bacon, remaining bacon grease with bread crumbs and seasoning. Refrigerate in a covered bowl overnight so flavor of bacon and seasoning mixes well with bread. (Richard says his secret ingredient is a poultry seasoning that is sold only in the East. But a little imagination on the part of any cook can improvise to make a flavorful dressing with the use of *her* favorite seasonings.)

On morning of the holiday cook goose giblets, chop and add to bread mixture. Lightly sauté mushrooms, cucumber and onion in oil. Add bread crumbs and fry together for about 10 minutes. This stuffing will fill a 14-pound goose.

Season cavity of goose with salt and pepper. Stuff loosely. Cover goose with sweet butter slathered on with spatula or spread with spoon. Roast according to size (approximately 4¾ hours for a 14-pound goose) in shallow roaster in slow oven (325°). Render fat every 15 minutes.

Sweet Potatoes With Marshmallows

4 medium sweet potatoes, cooked and peeled
½ teaspoon salt
½ cup brown sugar
½ cup butter
1 cup miniature marshmallows

Cut sweet potatoes into thick slices. Season potatoes with salt. In a small baking dish alternately layer potatoes, sugar, butter and marshmallows, omitting the final layer of marshmallows (reserve). Bake for 30 minutes, or until just done, in a preheated 350° oven. Add reserved marshamallows during last few minutes of baking; allow to brown and melt slightly before serving. (Serves 4)

At Mary Elizabeth's house the best things about both Thanksgiving and Christmas dinners are the delicious family specialties her mother prepares.

Turkey Dinner

Traditional Roast Turkey
Cornbread Stuffing*
Sweet Potatoes
Whipped Potatoes
Fresh Cranberries*
Green Salad
Pumpkin Pie with Yellow Crust*

* recipes given

Cornbread Stuffing

1-2 onions, minced
1 cup sliced celery
2 tablespoons cooking oil
16 cups combined bread cubes, cornbread cubes and baking powder biscuit cubes
¼ cup wheat germ

(optional)
4 eggs, beaten
¾ cup melted butter
1 teaspoon salt
2 teaspoons celery salt
¼ teaspoon freshly ground pepper
1½ teaspoons sage
1½ cups turkey stock

Sauté onion and celery in oil. Set aside. Combine bread crumbs and add raw wheat germ, if desired (Mrs. McDonough adds wheat germ to foods whenever possible). Add eggs, butter, salt, celery salt, pepper and sage. Mix well. Add turkey stock and toss again until bread is well coated.

Season cavity of turkey. Stuff and truss. Roast your favorite way. (Makes enough stuffing for a 14-pound bird)

Mrs. McDonough cooks fresh cranberries with a few drops of artificial sweetener instead of sugar. She says her family (especially Mary) likes the taste. Be careful not to add too much sweetener as it will make the cranberries taste bitter.

Pumpkin Pie With Yellow Crust

Make pie filling according to directions on can.

CRUST
½ cup yellow shortening
5 tablespoons hot water
Few drops milk
1½ cups sifted all-purpose flour
½ teaspoon salt

Whip together shortening and hot water. Add milk and whip again until smooth. In a separate bowl sift flour and salt. Cut in shortening. When mixture resembles cornmeal or small peas start forming into ball. Turn out on a floured board and flatten. Roll out to desired thickness to cover pie. Bake according to directions on can of pumpkin pie filling. (Makes 9-inch pie crust)

Christmas is a time for families to be together. The Walmsley's are a very close knit unit. Although they have many friends who invite them to share Christmas dinner, it's a time when the three of them spend a quiet day at home.

There are gifts to open; conversation to share and

lots of good food. Especially the turkey stuffing and desserts, according to Jon.

Jon's Favorite Holiday Dinner

Turkey with Stuffing
Sweet Potatoes
Mashed Potatoes
Corn
Mince Pie
Christmas Cake*
Fruit Whip*

* recipes given

Christmas Cake

Sift together in a medium-sized bowl:

3 cups all-purpose flour
2 level teaspoons mixed spices (cinnamon, nutmeg and allspice)
2 level teaspoons baking powder
Pinch salt

In second bowl mix together:

8 ounces currants
8 ounces raisins
8 ounces glazed cherries
4 ounces mixed orange and lemon peel
2 ounces chopped almonds
1 ounce brandy or sherry (optional)

Cream together in a separate bowl:

12 ounces butter or margarine
 8 ounces sugar
 6 eggs

Add eggs one at a time, beating well and adding 1–2 tablespoons of flour between each addition.

Blend fruit into butter/egg mixture. Fold in flour, a small amount at a time, mixing thoroughly so well blended. If mixture is stiff add milk until cake-batter consistency is right.

Grease a 9-inch springform pan. Turn batter into pan, level off if too full. Bake in 315° oven for 4 hours. Cool cake on wire rack in pan before removing. Decorate with favorite holiday icing, such as 7-minute whipped cream or lemon or vanilla glaze, and maraschino cherries. Add a sprig of holly if desired.

Fruit Whip

Cooked custard (see below), cooled
Fruit-filled gelatin
Whipped cream

GELATIN

Make strawberry gelatin according to package directions. When beginning to set add fruit of your choice (Jon likes mandarin oranges and peaches). Return to refrigerator until set.

CUSTARD
4 eggs, well beaten
¼ cup sugar
¼ teaspoon salt
3 cups hot milk
1 teaspoon vanilla extract

Combine eggs, sugar and salt in top of double boiler. Stir milk in slowly while cooking over boiling water. Continue stirring until mixture thickens to custard consistency. Add vanilla and mix through. Chill thoroughly in the same pot.

When sufficiently chilled pour custard over gelatin mixture. Cover with layer of whipped cream or whipped cream topping. (Serves 4)

An assortment of aunts, uncles and cousins gather at the home of Eric Scott for holiday dinners. His favorite one is Passover when the traditional Passover meal is served and the adults explain the meaning of this very important Jewish holiday. (Thanksgiving is Eric's second favorite.)

There are usually around 22 people gathered at the Scott table and the women in the family go all out in preparing mouth-watering dishes. For Eric it's a time of family closeness; of laughter, lively conversation and plenty of unbeatable food to eat.

Passover Dinner

Chicken Liver Spread (*see recipe on page 10*)
Stuffed Cabbage (*see recipe on page 7*) Sweet 'n Sour
Chicken Soup With Matzo Balls (*see recipe on page 41*)
Roast Chicken
Salad
Tzimmes*
Steamed Zucchini or Green Beans
Cold Fruit Compote*
Macaroons
Angel Food Cake (*see recipe on page 140*)

* recipes given

Tzimmes

½ cup unsweetened pitted prunes
1 cup cold water
2 large yams, peeled and cubed
2 large carrots, pared and sliced
1 red apple, cored and cubed
Honey to taste (¼ -½ cup)

Soak prunes in cold water for 30 minutes. Pour into a saucepan and bring to a boil. Add yams and carrots, cover, and simmer for 20 minutes. Add apple and honey to taste. Cover and cook an additional 25 minutes over a low flame. (If necessary add small amount of boiling water to prevent burning.)

Turn mixture into an oven-proof dish and bake in a preheated 300° oven for 20 minutes. (Serves 6)

Cold Fruit Compote

4 peaches, peeled and sliced
6 apricots, peeled and sliced
1 8-ounce can pineapple cubes, juice reserved
½ cup seedless grapes
½ cup honey
¼ cup white wine (optional)

Put all fruit in a medium-sized bowl. Blend pineapple juice with honey and wine. Pour over fruit. Cover with plastic wrap and chill for several hours. (Serves 6–8)

Judy and her family usually spend Christmas with very close family friends. They've been celebrating this special holiday together for years. But there are other occasions for special dinners. Sometimes Judy helps her mother prepare a holiday or company dinner. One of their favorites is individual Rock Cornish hens with a delicious sauce.

Orange/Sherry Birds

Salt to taste
  6 Rock Cornish hens
Freshly ground pepper (optional)
½ cup oil
¼ cup sherry
 1 cup orange juice
Dash ginger
 2 tablespoons brown sugar

Salt cavity of hens. Sprinkle with small amount of pepper, if desired. Mix together remaining ingredients. Place hens in shallow baking dish. With pastry brush baste hens with sauce. Bake in a preheated 325° oven until done, about 1 hour, basting every 10 minutes with sauce. (Serves 6)

With this the Nortons enjoy homemade cranberry relish.

Cranberry Relish

4 cups fresh cranberries
2 small oranges, quartered and seeded
2 cups sugar
1 cup finely chopped walnuts

Grind raw cranberries. Add other ingredients and mix well. Chill for 2–4 hours. (Makes 4–6 cups relish)

10

Miscellaneous Favorites

There's always a houseful of kids at the McDonough's. Mary shares a room with her 10-year-old sister Elaine. Both girls love to have friends over to spend the night. Mary's parents try very hard to keep her life as normal as possible and entertaining friends is an important part of her life. It's not unusual to find sleeping bags spread out on the floor of the living room where an impromptu pajama party is taking place.

Both of Mary's brothers are basketball players. Sixteen year old John is 6'4" and 19 year old Mike is 6'3". Family entertaining often centers around high school basketball games or high school plays. Afterwards the McDonoughs, their four children and "friends" have a great time indulging in a favorite pastime, eating homemade ice cream.

There are peach trees all around their home in Northridge, a suburb of Los Angeles, and strawberries grow out in front. Whenever they want ice cream they haul out the electric mixer, gather up fresh fruit and mix up a fresh batch of creamy peach or mouth-watering strawberry ice cream.

Homemade Ice Cream

CUSTARD BASE

2 cups milk	1½ teaspoons vanilla
3 egg yolks	extract
1 cup sugar	2 cups heavy cream
½ teaspoon salt	2 cups puréed fruit

Scald milk in top part of double boiler. Beat egg yolks with sugar, salt and blend with milk. Cook over hot, but not boiling, water until thickened. Remove from heat and cover with wax paper. Chill.

Stir in vanilla and cream. Blend and add puréed fruit. Pour into freezer container of ice cream maker and follow manufacturer's directions for best results. (Makes 1 quart ice cream)

If you don't have an ice cream freezer, electric or hand crank, you can still turn out great home-made ice cream right in the freezer compartment of your refrigerator.

Refrigerator Ice Cream

Prepare Custard Base as directed (see above). Add vanilla. Pour into an ice tray (without cube dividers) and freeze for about 1 hour, or until mushy. Whip cream until stiff peaks form. In a wet-chilled bowl beat custard mixture until smooth. Fold in whipped cream and fruit. Pour into freezer containers to about 1 inch from the top. Freeze, covered, for 1 hour during which time stir often. Freeze, undisturbed, for 3–4 hours more. Should make about 1 quart of yummy ice cream, free of preservatives and packed with good nutrition.

Puddings are a favorite side dish or light dessert with many of the Waltons.

Jon's mom often serves this to top off a light supper.

Steamed Pudding

- 2 cups self-rising flour or 2 cups all-purpose flour with 1 teaspoon baking powder
- ½ teaspoon salt
- 4 tablespoons butter or margarine
- 2 tablespoons sugar
- 3 tablespoons milk or 1 egg (depending on richness you prefer)

Cream together butter or margarine and sugar. Mix flour and salt and blend in butter. Add 2 tablespoons of any of the following:

Marmalade
Jam
Currants
Raisins
Dates (pitted and cut up)

Blend thoroughly with flour mixture, add egg or milk and mix through. Pour into a well greased bowl. Set bowl in pot with about 2 inches of boiling water. Cover and steam for 2–2½ hours. Serve with sweetened white sauce or custard sauce.

Kami's mom makes super crêpes, the real French dessert that tastes so scrumptious. It's a great party treat, too.

Crêpes Suzette

1 cup all-purpose flour combined with a pinch of salt
1 tablespoon sugar
2 cups milk (or 1 cup milk and 1 cup water for a lighter crêpe)
4 eggs, beaten until frothy and light in color
2 tablespoons melted butter

Sift flour into a bowl. Add sugar. In a separate bowl blend milk with eggs. Gradually add to flour mixture, beating until smooth. Add melted butter. Refrigerate for 1 hour, or until batter is the consistency of heavy cream.

Heat a 5-or 6-inch skillet or crêpe pan until a drop of water dances on it. Brush with butter. Ladle in 1½ tablespoons of batter. Tilt rapidly, rotating pan to spread batter evenly. Cook for 1 minute, or until edges are light brown. Turn and cook on other side. Crêpes should have a lacy look. Spread on towel and keep warm until crêpes are ready for sauce. (Makes 2–2½ dozen)

Fold crêpes first into halves and then into quarters. They will look like squares with flaps. Mrs. Cotler prepares a rich butter sauce flavored with orange and lemon peels and liqueurs and heats it well.

SAUCE:

½ cup sweet butter
½ cup mixed orange and lemon peels
⅓ cup brandy
2 tablespoons rum
¼ cup Cointreau

In chafing dish melt butter on low flame. Add liqueurs, orange and lemon peels. Heat through.

Add crêpes to sauce in chafing dish and spoon sauce over crêpes until well saturated. Serve piping hot sprinkled with confectioners' sugar.

At the McDonough's Sunday means pancakes with freshly picked strawberries. Strawberries also mean homemade jam to spread on freshly baked bread or biscuits. Her mom's homemade jam is what Mary likes in a sandwich with natural peanut butter.

Homemade Strawberry Jam

4½ cups ripe strawberries
1 box powdered fruit pectin
7 cups sugar
11 6-8 ounce sterile glasses
hot paraffin

Crush strawberries, small amount at a time. Put in a large saucepan, add pectin and mix well. Bring to a hard boil, stirring constantly, over high flame. Add sugar immediately after mixture starts to boil. Bring to full rolling boil, stirring constantly for 1 minute.

Remove from heat and skim off foam with metal spoon. Continue to alternately stir and skim for about 5 minutes to cool slightly and to prevent fruit from floating. Ladle quickly into well sterilized glasses or jars. Cover jam with ⅛ inch of hot melted paraffin.

For a special luncheon treat or as an accompaniment to a fish dinner Eric Scott's family love blintzes. The batter is very similar to that of a crêpe, but the pancakes are larger.

Cheese Blintzes

BATTER
2 eggs
1 cup cold water
1 cup all-purpose flour

Beat eggs well in a bowl. Add 1/3 cup of the water and mix thoroughly. Add ¼ cup of the flour slowly, stirring constantly. Alternate flour with water as above. Refrigerate for 30 minutes.

FILLING
1 pound hoop cheese (buy in deli section of supermarket)
1 egg
¼ cup sugar
Dash salt
Dash vanilla or cinnamon (optional)

In a small bowl blend cheese with egg. Add sugar and salt, blending all ingredients thoroughly. If desired, a dash of vanilla or cinnamon may be added and mixed through.

To make blintzes heat a 10-inch frying pan. Melt 2 tablespoons of butter until bottom of pan is well coated. Pour about 3–4 tablespoons batter, tilting pan until bottom of pan is well coated. Cook over medium heat until underside of blintze is light brown. Turn onto a clean dish towel, brown side up.

When all blintzes have been made place 1½ tablespoons of cheese mixture onto each pancake (the side that has been browned).

Fold each blintze into a four-corner square or roll up. Fry in melted butter until golden brown. (Makes 12 blintzes)

Serve piping hot . . .

1. With spoonful of sour cream on top of each blintze.
2. Sprinkled with confectioners' sugar or cinnamon
3. With ice cold applesauce
4. Topped with strawberry or cherry jam

Earl Hamner, Jr. and his family lived in apple country. Winchester, Virginia, was the center of Governor Byrd's renowned apple orchards. Even during the depression, if you lived near the county seat as the Hamners did, apples were very easy to come by. As Earl remembers, "You could buy bushels of delicious winesaps for very little money."

His mother, he recalls, made a variety of good tasting treats from apples. "One of my best memories of those days is the aroma of food cooking."

Mrs. Hamner would slice up a bowl of apples and set them out to dry. Then she would serve them wrapped in crêpe dough. In this modern age you have only to go to your local market and buy a package of dried apples to serve your family a healthy, savory treat.

Dried Apple Crepes

Makes crêpes as for Crêpes Suzette (see recipe on page 119).

FILLING
2 cups dried apples
Cinnamon sugar
Butter
Cinnamon

Fill each crêpe with 4 slices of apple. Sprinkle with cinnamon sugar. Roll up, dot with butter, sprinkle with plain cinnamon and bake in a preheated 350° oven for about 30 minutes, or until heated through. (Serves 6)

Applesauce

6 red apples
½ cup water (or to cover)
½ cup sugar (or to taste depending upon tartness of apples)

Peel and core apples. Cut into thick slices. In a large saucepan cook apples with water until they start to get soft. Gradually stir in sugar to taste. Cover and simmer over a very low flame until apples are soft and mushy. Press through a sieve into a bowl. Chill until ready to serve.

If you like applesauce with a bit of color add few drops of red food coloring for a rosy hue. For a tart flavor add 1–2 teaspoons of lemon juice when cooking apples.

Sugar-cured ham, freshly laid eggs and hot oven biscuits was the kind of substantial breakfast served in the Hamner household. Sometimes the family would come down to the kitchen and find it fragrant with the sweet aroma of fried apple rings that Mrs. Hamner was preparing to go along with their usual breakfast fare.

Fried Apple Rings

4 medium apples, washed and cored
Brown sugar
4 tablespoons butter

Cut apples in half-inch rings. Sprinkle with brown sugar. Melt butter in a hot frying pan. Sauté apples until light brown and tender, turning to fry on both sides. An absolutely unbeatable side dish with ham or pork.

No doubt about it, Mrs. Hamner was very inventive in her cooking. "We lived simply, and had few products," Earl says of that era. "But my mother would make different uses of whatever we did have."

Apple Pancakes

1½ cups sifted all-purpose flour	1 egg, unbeaten
3 teaspoons baking powder	1 cup milk
½ teaspoon cinnamon	2 cups finely chopped apples (peeled and cored)
¾ teaspoon salt	Deep fat for frying

Sift dry ingredients together in a bowl. In a separate bowl combine egg, milk and apples. Add to dry ingredients. Mix to moisten.

In an electric fryer or deep fat fryer heat fat until 350°. Drop a heaping tablespoonful of batter for each pancake. Fry until golden brown on both sides. Drain well on paper towels. (Serves 12—2 pancakes per person)

Hot Apple/Noodle Pudding

1 pound package wide noodles (Earl's mom made her own)	apples
	½ cup yellow raisins
Small jar apple butter	¼ cup chopped walnuts
1 cup pared diced fresh	¼ pound sweet butter
	Dash cinnamon

Cook noodles in boiling salted water until tender. Drain well. In a large bowl mix hot noodles with apple butter, apples, raisins, and walnuts.

Melt sweet butter in 8 x 10 square baking dish. Pour in noodle mixture. Dot with additional butter or a small amount of apple butter. Sprinkle with cinnamon. Bake in a preheated 350° oven for 1 hour, or until well browned on top. Serve hot with turkey or other poultry.

If you've never tasted the delicate flavor of fried bananas, Richard Thomas told us, then you're in for a real taste pleaser. Richard first was introduced to this delightful dish when he was just a little boy touring Cuba with his parents, who now operate the New York School of Ballet. In Cuba they grow a fruit much like the banana called, the platano.

Fried Bananas or *Platano Frito*

4 ripe bananas
Melted butter
Confectioners' sugar or grated coconut (optional)

Slice the banana thickly. Heat butter in a skillet. Fry banana slices on both sides until golden brown, drain. May be sprinkled with confectioners sugar or shredded coconut if desired before serving. (Serves 4)

Bananas are a favorite with Richard. For years he would anticipate his family's infrequent visits to New Orleans. One of the reasons was that his very favorite dessert is served only in Brennans, a New Orleans restaurant. But recently very dear friends of his somehow wangled the recipe from someone and presented it to Richard as a Christmas present. The following is not an exact replica of Brennan's fabulous desert, but with a bit of practice you can produce your own spectacular at home.

Bananas Foster

3 tablespoons sweet butter
¾ cup superfine brown sugar
¼ cup banana liqueur
1 banana per person
1 scoop vanilla ice cream

Melt butter in skillet over medium heat taking care not to burn. Add sugar gradually, stirring until melted and syrupy. Remove from heat. Add banana liqueur and blend well.

Slice bananas. Heat in saucepan with liqueur mixture, basting frequently. When piping hot pour over ice cream and forget your diet.

Not too long ago Earl Hamner, Jr. was in New York dining at a very famous restaurant where unusual wild game foods, at very expensive prices, are featured exclusively on the menu. He was surprised and even a little amused to find a dish he and his family had often enjoyed during the difficult depression days priced at $50 per serving.

Living in the country with Nature at their fingertips the fact that times were hard everywhere was evident in the lack of money for luxuries and sometimes even for necessities. But there was good food to be grown on the land, or hunted and fished for in the nearby mountains and lakes. Earl recalls that often his father would go off hunting in an area where there were coveys of quail. He would bring back enough for the family to have for breakfast the next day.

"My father would dress them the night before. The next morning my mother would stew them in a big pot and make a really good flour gravy. Then with her fresh hot biscuits it would be a fantastic morning meal."

11

Goodies

---

*We've saved the best for the last. Doesn't every-
one crave a sweet treat now and then? This is the
chapter that has them. For starters here's the cake
made famous on "The Waltons." It's made from an
old family recipe and has often been mentioned on
the television series. Happy nibbling!*

Mrs. Hamner's Applesauce Cake

3½ cups sifted all-
   purpose flour
1 teaspoon soda
Pinch salt
1 teaspoon cinnamon
2 teaspoons ground
   cloves
2 teaspoons nutmeg

1 cup chopped black
   walnuts
2 cups light raisins
1 cup butter
1 cup sugar
2 eggs
2 cups applesauce

Sift together flour, soda, salt, cinnamon, cloves and nutmeg. Blend ½ cup flour, mixture with nuts and raisins. Set both mixtures aside.

Cream butter until soft and light. Gradually add sugar, beating until mixture is smooth. Beat in eggs vigorously. Alternately stir in 3 cups flour mixture and applesauce mixing well with each addition.

Add raisin/nut mixture. Grease a 3-quart cake mold. Pour in cake batter and bake in preheated oven at 350° for 1 hour.

Cool in pan for 10 minutes. Turn out on cake rack.

Although his mother served her applesauce cake just as it came from the oven, Earl Hamner's wife, an excellent cook in her own right, whipped together a very interesting icing for this very special cake.

Jane's Whiskey Frosting

¼ cup butter
2 cups confectioners' sugar
Pinch salt
1 tablespoon cream
2 tablespoons bourbon

Cream butter. Add sugar and salt gradually. Add cream and bourbon. Whip until smooth. Frost cooled cake. Decorate with sprig of holly.

Most men enjoy a good coffeecake. Here's one that Ralph Waite gave his seal of approval, though he admitted that he tries not to eat rich foods except on occasion.

Mink's Coffeecake

½ cup plus 2 tablespoons butter
2 teaspoons cinnamon
1 cup brown sugar
1 cup chopped nuts
2 cups sifted flour
1 teaspoon baking powder
1 teaspoon soda
¾ cup granulated sugar
1 teaspoon vanilla extract
3 eggs
1 cup sour cream

In a small bowl soften 2 tablespoons butter and cream with cinnamon and brown sugar. Add nuts and set aside.

In a separate bowl sift flour, baking powder and soda. Cream the 1½ cup butter. Add granulated sugar gradually, mixing well. Add vanilla and beat thoroughly. Add eggs, one at a time, beating well after each addition.

Add a small amount of flour mixture to creamed mixture alternately with sour cream and blend well. Continue until all flour and sour cream are used.

Pour half the cake mixture into greased 10-inch tube cake pan. Add half the nut mixture. Add remaining cake batter and top with remaining nut mixture.

Bake in a preheated 350° oven for about 40-45 minutes. Test with toothpick. If it comes out clean then cake is done. (1 10-inch tube cake)

Mary Elizabeth adds a lot of goodies to her oat-meal cookie recipe.

All Together Oatmeal Cookies

½ cup shortening	½ teaspoon ground cinnamon
¾ cup brown sugar	
1 egg	½ teaspoon nutmeg
¼ cup buttermilk	1½ cups quick oats
1 scant cup all-purpose flour, sifted	½ cup dark raisins
	½ cup chocolate chips
½ teaspoon soda	¼ cup chopped walnuts
½ teaspoon baking powder	

Cream shortening with brown sugar. Add egg and beat until fluffy. Stir in buttermilk. Sift dry ingredients together and stir gradually into creamed mixture. Add oats, raisins, chocolate chips and nuts.

Drop onto a lightly greased cookie sheet, about 1 tablespoon for each cookie, 2 inches apart. Bake for 10 minutes in a preheated 400° oven.

Cool slightly and remove from sheet. (Makes about 2½ dozen, cookies)

Despite a hectic schedule that includes ballet lessons, Mary enjoys domestic chores such as cooking and baking. Whenever possible she likes to bake something special for her family and often helps her mother with the wedding cakes that Mrs. McDonough bakes as gifts for very close friends whose children or grandchildren are getting married.

Mary's Carrot Cake

2 cups all-purpose flour
1 teaspoon soda
1½ cups sugar
½ teaspoon salt
2 teaspoons cinnamon
4 eggs
3 cups fresh carrot pulp (shredded carrots) with enough carrot juice to moisten
1 cup salad oil
1 cup shredded coconut
1 cup pecans

Sift flour with soda, sugar, salt and cinnamon. In a separate bowl mix eggs, carrot pulp and oil. In a large bowl alternately mix flour and carrot mixtures. Add coconut and pecans and mix through until thoroughly blended. Grease and flour an 8-inch square pan. Pour in cake batter and bake in a preheated 350° oven for 40 minutes.

FROSTING
4 ounces cream cheese, softened or whipped
1 teaspoon butter
1 cup confectioners' sugar
¼ cup orange juice
½ tablespoon grated orange peel

Blend cream cheese with butter. Cream in sugar. When well mixed add orange juice gradually until frosting becomes spreadable. Add orange peel and mix through just before frosting warm cake. (Allow to cool for 15 minutes after removing from oven.

Four- or Five-Tier Wedding Cake

3 cups sugar	1 cup shortening
8 egg whites	2 cups milk
2 teaspoons salt	1½ teaspoons orange
2 tablespoons baking	extract
powder	1 teaspoon almond
5¼ cups sifted cake flour	extract

Add 1 cup sugar to egg whites that have been beaten. Add salt and baking powder to flour in a separate bowl. Cream remaining 2 cups sugar with shortening in a small bowl. Blend dry ingredients with shortening a small amount at a time, mixing well after each addition. Add milk gradually and blend so flour is dampened. Beat on low speed of electric mixer for 2 minutes. Add orange and almond extracts and mix through. Fold in meringue.

Line bottom of 8-inch cake pans with wax paper. Divide batter equally between the pans. Bake in a preheated slow oven (325°) for about 45 minutes, or until done.

LEMON FILLING

½ cup sugar	1 tablespoon grated
2 tablespoons cornstarch	lemon peel
Dash salt	¼ cup lemon juice
½ cup water	Drop yellow food color
2 teaspoon butter	

Put dry ingredients that have been well mixed into a saucepan. Gradually stir in water and cook, stirring constantly, until mixture thickens and starts to boil. Allow to boil for 1 minute. Remove immediately from heat. Blend in butter and lemon peel. Add lemon juice and food coloring and mix thoroughly. Allow to cool before filling between cake layers.

Frost wedding cake with plain white icing. Decorate as desired.

Another delicious cake that Mary is learning to bake is

A Good Banana-Nut Cake

1⅔ cups sugar (the McDonoughs use raw sugar)
⅔ cup shortening
2¼ cups cake flour
1¼ teaspoons soda
1¼ teaspoons baking powder
1 teaspoon salt
3 medium-sized ripe bananas, well mashed
⅔ cup buttermilk
3 eggs
¾ cup nuts (walnuts or pecans), chopped

Grease and flour a 9x13 oblong cake pan or 2 9-inch cake rounds. Preheat oven to 350°.

Cream sugar with shortening. Sift in dry ingredients. Beat together for about 3-4 minutes. Add mashed banana and buttermilk alternately, mixing well after each addition. Blend in eggs and beat an additional 2 minutes. Fold in nuts.

Bake for 35 minutes.* Cool in pans for 10 minutes. Remove to cake rack. Cool completely before frosting with Sour Cream Butter Frosting (see pg 135).

* If using oblong pan increase baking time to 45-50 minutes.

Sour Cream-Butter Frosting

⅓ cup butter
2 pounds confectioners' sugar
½ teaspoon salt
2 teaspoons vanilla extract
¼-½ cup dairy sour cream
1-2 tablespoons milk (optional)

Cream butter with sugar. Add salt, vanilla and sour cream. Mix until ingredients are blended thoroughly and of a spreadable consistency. If necessary stir in 1 or 2 tablespoons of milk to bring to proper consistency.

Ellen Corby still considers this to be one of the best apple cakes ever baked. It's an old Danish recipe handed down through the family and served often in her mother's restaurant.

Aeblekage

2 cups unseasoned bread crumbs
2 cups homemade applesauce
Sugar as needed
½ cup melted butter

In 4-4½ inch rectangular baking dish layer as follows: bread crumbs (spread out to cover bottom of dish) applesauce, and sprinkle of sugar. Repeat, ending with a layer of breadcrumbs. Press together well with a spoon. Pour melted butter (add more if

necessary) over mix. Bake in a preheated 350° oven
for 30 minutes.

Cool in dish. Turn out when lukewarm and serve
with fresh icy cold, whipped cream. (Serves 4)

*At Kami's house it's a treat to eat when her mom
makes the pie she likes best.*

Grasshopper Pie

BOTTOM CRUST
24 Oreo cookies, finely crushed
¼ cup melted butter

Combine all but ½ cup cookie crumbs with
butter. Press into buttered 9-inch spring-form pan.
Set aside.

FILLING
¼ cup crème de menthe
1 pint jar marshmallow crème
2 cups heavy cream, whipped

Stir together gradually crème de menthe and
marshmallow crème. Mix until well blended. Fold
in whipped cream. Pour into pan with bottom crust.
Sprinkle with reserved crumbs. Put in freezer until
firm enough to cut. (Serves 8)

*The English have a special way with light des-
serts to be served at tea time or following a hearty
meal. Michael Learned spent some time in an
English boarding school during her teen years and*

this is one dessert she can't resist. It's a recipe Jon's mother uses often, for company and as a treat for her family.

English Trifle

SPONGE SANDWICH BASIS

3 eggs
½ cup sugar
1 cup all-purpose flour
1 level teaspoon baking powder
Pinch salt
Few drops vanilla
Strawberry jam

Beat eggs and sugar until light and fluffy. Sift dry ingredients and fold into egg mixture. Add vanilla. Mix thoroughly. Grease 2 8-inch loaf pans. Divide batter equally between the two pans. Bake in a preheated oven 350° for 25-30 minutes. (In meantime have custard made up and chilling in refrigerator).

When cool, remove from pans. Spread strawberry jam between layers and put together sandwich style. Set in rectangular dish and soak with fruit juice of your choice. Add small amount of sherry, if desired (this gives an additional subtle flavor). Let stand long enough for flavors to blend. Cut sandwich into large pieces. Put in individual dessert bowls.

Cover sponge sandwich with layer of custard. Top with whipped cream and sliced almonds. Chill well before serving. (Serves 6)

Scones are another English tea-time treat at the Walmsley's.

Rich Scones

2 cups self-rising flour
  or 2 cups all-purpose
  flour
½ teaspoon salt
1½ teaspoon butter or
  margarine
1 tablespoon sugar

2 tablespoons currants
1 egg, beaten (reserve
  1 tablespoon)
Milk
1 teaspoon baking
  powder

Mix flour and salt in a bowl. With fingertips lightly rub in butter. Add sugar and currants. Using dull knife stir in beaten egg and enough milk to form a soft dough.

Dough must be handled very lightly. Be careful not to overknead.

Roll dough out on flour board to a half-inch thickness. With floured round biscuit or cookie cutter cut out 2-inch rounds.

Place on greased baking sheet. Brush tops with reserved beaten egg using a pastry brush. Bake for 10 minutes in a preheated oven. 425–450°.

For a party Jon's mother will often bake up another sandwich type cake with less sponge to it, but just as delicious.

Party Cake

1 cup all-purpose flour	½ cup sugar
1 level teaspoon baking powder	2 eggs
Pinch salt	Vanilla extract
½ cup butter or margarine	Milk

Grease and flour 2 8-inch pans. Sprinkle with sugar.

Sift together the flour, baking powder and salt and cream the butter and sugar. Beat the eggs in with small amount of the sifted flour in separate bowl. Add a few drops of vanilla. Fold into flour and add enough milk to form a soft but not runny batter.

Pour batter into prepared pans. Bake for 20–25 minutes in a preheated 400° oven.

When cool sandwich together with jam mixed with small amount of sweet cream. Frost with chocolate icing. (Serves 12)

Angel Food Cake

1½ cups egg whites (about 12), at room temperature	1½ teaspoons cream of tartar
1 cup sifted cake flour	¼ teaspoon salt
1¼ cups confectioners' sugar	¼ cup sugar
	1½ teaspoons vanilla extract

Eggs should be separated when cold and allowed to stand, covered, until room temperature. Sift flour twice. In a small bowl mix together confectioners' sugar and flour. On high speed of electric mixer beat egg whites, cream of tartar, salt and vanilla in large bowl. Beat until moist and glossy but stiff enough to form peaks. Add sugar tablespoons at a time and do not scrape sides of bowl while beating. Sift a fourth of the flour mixture over egg whites and fold in. Continue to do this until all the flour is used.

Bake in an ungreased 10-inch tube pan in a preheated 375° oven for 35 minutes. Invert cake in pan and allow to cool completely before removing. For easy removal gently loosen cake from pan with metal spatula and turn onto plate.

Serve with sliced fresh strawberries, sprinkled with confectioners' sugar or topped with whipped cream. (Serves 12–16)

If there's any cake David Harper likes better than chocolate it's a chocolate one with chocolate frosting. Or maybe chocolate cake with chocolate ice cream, à la mode style.

Yummy Chocolate Loaf Cake

⅓ cup butter	1¼ cups sifted cake flour
½ cup sugar	½ teaspoon soda
½ teaspoon vanilla extract	¼ teaspoon salt
	¾ cup ice water
1 egg	1 cup (6-ounce package) semisweet chocolate pieces
1 3-ounce bar sweet cooking chocolate, melted and cooled	

Cream butter. Slowly add sugar and continue

creaming until light in texture. Add vanilla and egg, beating thoroughly. Blend in chocolate.

Sift cake flour with soda and salt. Add alternately with water to creamed mixture beating well after each addition.

Bake in a greased and floured 9x5x3-inch loaf pan in a preheated 350°oven for 35 minutes. While cake is still hot sprinkle top with chocolate bits and let them melt for an easy frosting.

At Christmas Judy bakes up batches of her favorite kinds of cookies, wraps them in tinfoil, packs them carefully in attractive baskets and delivers them to her friends.

Improvisational Cookies

Batch #1—More of a Candy . . .

2 cups confectioners' sugar
3 cups shredded coconut
½ cup butter, melted
2 1-ounce squares unsweetened chocolate, melted

Stir sugar and coconut into melted butter. Mix well and chill, covered, in refrigerator for about an hour. Shape into small balls and make slight indentation in center of each ball. Drizzle melted chocolate onto center. Chill again until firm. (Makes about 3 dozen goodies)

Batch #2—Fudge Squares

½ cup shortening
2 1-ounce squares un-
   sweetened chocolate
2 eggs
1 cup granulated sugar
1 teaspoon vanilla

extract or almond
flavoring
½ cup sifted all-purpose
flour
¼ teaspoon salt
½ cup seedless raisins
½ cup almond slivers

In the top of a double boiler melt shortening and chocolate over hot water. Cool. In separate bowl beat eggs and add sugar gradually, beating well after each addition. Blend chocolate mixture and vanilla with eggs. Gradually add flour and salt that have been sifted once. Add raisins and almonds.

Grease an 8-inch square pan and spread batter over bottom. Bake in a preheated 350° oven for 30 minutes. Cool in pan before cutting into small squares. (Makes about 2 dozen)

Batch #3—Peanut Butter Chocos

¼ cup butter
¼ cup peanut butter
¼ cup granulated sugar
¼ cup brown sugar
1 egg
¼ teaspoon vanilla
   extract

¾ cup sifted all-purpose
flour
Dash salt
2 ounces semisweet
chocolate chips

Cream together butter, peanut butter, sugars, egg and vanilla. Gradually blend sifted dry ingredients with butter mixture. Add chocolate chips and mix together so chips are distributed evenly throughout cookie batter.

Shape into small balls and place on an ungreased

cookie sheet allowing at least 2 inches between cookies for spreading. Bake for 10–12 minutes at 375°. Cool before removing from pan. (Makes 2 dozen)

For a holiday extra Judy decorates her cookies and candies with colored sprinkles.

At the Scott's the cookie that everyone loves is really different.

Gumdrop Hermits

1 cup colored gumdrops (eliminate black ones)
1½ cups all-purpose flour
2 teaspoons baking powder
½ teaspoon salt
1 teaspoon cinnamon
½ cup shortening
1 cup sugar
1 egg, well beaten
1 teaspoon vanilla extract
¼ cup milk

Cut gumdrops into very small pieces. Set aside.

Sift flour, remeasure exact amount and add baking powder, salt and cinnamon. Sift again.

In a medium bowl cream shortening. Add sugar a small amount at a time and cream until light. Add egg and blend thoroughly. Stir in vanilla and gumdrops.

Add dry ingredients alternately with milk. Mix well. Drop by teaspoonsful onto a greased cookie sheet. Bake for 12–14 minutes at 350°. (Makes 3 dozen)

Index

ABOUT THE AUTHOR

SYLVIA RESNICK, a former associate editor of Rona Barrett's *Hollywood* magazine, has written on the Hollywood scene as a celebrity interviewer and gossip columnist for twelve years. Currently, she writes on cuisine, health and nutrition, beauty and travel for national magazines. Her favorite hobby is collecting and testing recipes. In addition to *The Walton Family Cookbook*, she researched *The Partridge Family Cookbook*. Mrs. Resnick lives in Canoga Park, California, with her husband and son.